Date Due

DEC 14			
NOV 24			
Mar 2			
APR 19			
MAY 5			
NOV 16			
NOV 30			
OCT 27			
MAY 8			
MAY 16			

No. 293   DEMCO-MADISON-WIS

TOLSTOY AND HIS WIFE

TOLSTOY
AND
HIS WIFE

By TIKHON POLNER

Translated by NICHOLAS WREDEN

W · W · NORTON & COMPANY · INC · *New York*

Copyright, 1945, by
W. W. NORTON & COMPANY, INC.
70 Fifth Avenue, New York 11, N. Y.

First Edition

A WARTIME BOOK

THIS COMPLETE EDITION IS PRODUCED IN
FULL COMPLIANCE WITH THE GOVERN-
MENT'S REGULATIONS FOR CONSERVING
PAPER AND OTHER ESSENTIAL MATERIALS.

PRINTED IN THE UNITED STATES OF AMERICA

Translator's Note

DURING the grim, trying years of war the Russian people and their leaders in their search for spiritual anchors became keenly aware of their national heritage. A great revival of interest in pre-Revolutionary history and literature swept over Russia, and made itself felt in every part of the world where men and women watched with admiration the heroic defense of their homeland by the Russians. In their effort to share and understand the sources of inner strength that had sustained the Russians in their trial, people everywhere spontaneously turned to the greatest Russian national epic—Tolstoy's *War and Peace*— which is a panorama of another critical period in the life of the Russian people.

Just as a current phase of a nation's history is a logical sequence of everything that went before, so a great novel is invariably the projection of the writer's experiences and antecedents. As I reread *War and Peace,* and as I watched thousands of other people read it, my thoughts turned more and more often to a book that had appeared in Russian in Paris during the late 1920's. *Tolstoy and His Wife* by Tikhon Polner made me more aware of Tolstoy as a human being than anything else I have ever read. At the time Tikhon Polner and I exchanged several letters, and he gave me his permission to translate the book into English. I made a rough first draft of a translation, then came the depression, the press of hard work, and the manuscript was put away into a box. But with the resurgence of interest in Russian literature and particularly in Tolstoy, I once again felt a desire to make this book available to the English-speaking public.

To me *Tolstoy and His Wife* is at once a fine interpretive biography, and a touchingly human story. In a peculiar way it is also a connecting link between the past and the present.

Tikhon Polner was a typical public-spirited liberal in pre-Revolutionary Russia. He was a product of the same education and of the same environment that produced Tolstoy. To him the problem of writing this book was not one of academic research. Rather it was one of exercising restraint and good judgment in interpreting the character of a great man, and in telling the personal story of two people whom he loved and admired. *Tolstoy and His Wife* could have been written only by a contemporary and a friend.

N. W.

New York City
January 1, 1945

> N.B.—The dates in this book are given in accordance with the Julian Calendar, which was still in use in Russia during the period covered.

Chapter One

IT IS hard to picture the excitement under which Russia was laboring in the late 1850's. Among the better-educated classes liberal opinions had been ripening for some time. But in the name of Russia's might, these tendencies had been kept down by the heavy hand of the reactionary regime of Nicholas I. The prosecution of "red" ideas had become especially acute in connection with the revolutionary wave that rolled over Europe in 1848. The government had understood that many of the old Russian institutions no longer answered the people's needs. Peasant serfdom was one of them. Slowly, with the greatest possible secrecy, reforms were prepared in the government offices in Petersburg; but such abundant self-assurance had reigned at the top, that even the officials preparing them had no faith in their work.

The fall of Sevastopol put an end to this self-assurance. Very frequently war is more than a test in the art of diplomacy and wartime efficiency. It tests the entire governmental structure and mercilessly destroys proud illusions.

The Russian government failed to pass the test presented by the siege of Sevastopol. Russia's might, for which so much had been sacrificed, proved to be a myth. Among society people rumors persisted that Emperor Nicholas, unable to face the downfall of his governmental system, had committed suicide. Hopes as lovely as the rainbow centered around the name of his heir. A pupil of the poet Zhukovsky, sensitive and tender, Alexander II seemed to be sent by heaven to heal Russia's deep wounds, to make her forget the stern regime of his father, and to lead her on the path of reconstruction.

Murmurs of dissatisfaction, which had been held down with great effort toward the end of the preceding reign, now came to the surface. Among the enslaved peasants discontent reached un-

precedented proportions. After a long-enforced silence the liberal-
minded were on the offensive. The dike broke and an ocean of
political literature burst through the opening. In characteristic
Russian fashion everything was criticized. Everything was bad.
Everything had to be changed immediately: serfdom, courts, public education, censorship, local government. Many already had
hopes for a "complete edifice," that is, a written constitution.
There did not seem to be names enough for the new magazines
and newspapers. Problems (a term used in 1856 for any com-
bination of circumstances that no one understood) appeared from
all directions. Problems connected with military academies, universities, censorship, jury trials, finances, banks, the police, emancipation, and everything else. Everyone was looking for new problems. Everyone was trying to solve them. Everyone was writing,
reading, talking, and planning. Everyone wanted to make changes
and improvements—to turn things upside down. "All Russians,
as one man, were in perpetual throes of enthusiasm," Lev Tolstoy
wrote sarcastically some time later.

The country was tearing down its patriarchal foundations,
which had outlived their usefulness, and was entering a new
phase of development in the economic field. The kettle was boil-
ing, and public life, at last finding its way into the open, was
shining with all the colors of a rainbow. Its very tempo and its
complexities were certain to affect everyone.

2

In November, 1855, a young army officer appeared in Petersburg
and created a furor. He arrived as a military courier, bringing
dispatches concerning the last bombardment of Sevastopol. The
young man proved to be a tremendous success in all the social
coteries of the capital. Later he wrote, "All the lights of society
sought my acquaintance, shook my hand, proffered dinner en-
gagements, persisted in making me accept invitations. . . ." This
reception was attributable neither to his military achievements
nor to his rank. Though physically brave, he had not had an

opportunity to display his courage. He was known because, during the three preceding years, his name had appeared in the leading magazines. When he was twenty-four and serving as an artillery cadet in the wilds of the Caucasus, he finished *Childhood,* an autobiographical sketch which he had begun while living in Moscow. Signed with initials that no one knew, this sketch appeared in the September, 1852, issue of the *Sovremennik,* a very popular magazine edited by the poet Nekrasov. Readers were charmed by his characterizations, by his simplicity, his warmth, his sincerity, and his unusual sensitivity. *The Invaders, Boyhood, Recollections of a Marker, The Wood-cutting Expedition, Sevastopol in December,* and *Sevastopol in May* appeared between 1853 and 1855. The last two made a particularly strong impression. At that time the whole people's attention centered on Sevastopol. From the imperial family down to the last laborer, Russia wept over these Sevastopol stories, which pictured the Russian soldier with truth and simplicity. The reading public already recognized the rising star of Russian literature. The fame of Count Lev Tolstoy was made and grew with unbelievable speed. He had barely entered the field of letters, and he already had no equals. The well-known novelist and playwright Pisemsky, reading Tolstoy's stories, sternly said, "This upstart of an officer will make short work of us all. One almost feels like throwing away the pen." The reserved and dry Nekrasov wrote to Tolstoy in September, 1855, "I know of no writer who makes one feel as much love and sympathy for him, as the one I am addressing." With delight Turgenev read his friends the unknown author's stories.

It was to Turgenev's apartment that Tolstoy went immediately on his arrival in Petersburg, and it was there that he lived during the first part of his stay. They both sincerely wanted to know each other better. But their spheres were entirely too far apart.

As a matter of fact they had very little in common. Turgenev was ten years older and, to a great extent, he had lived down the turbulence of youth. Soft, easily influenced (especially by women), at times sharp tongued, extremely civilized, an admirer of the scientific schools of the West and of their liberal tendencies, Turgenev believed in the educational value of political institutions, and was wholeheartedly in favor of the proposed reforms. He enjoyed his popularity, sought followers among the young, and tried to keep himself at the height of scientific and literary fashion. His soul was not eternally tormented by the "damned problems" of human existence. He was certain that he was doing his share. The social work performed by Turgenev, and by the group of liberal-minded authors who centered around the *Sovremennik,* was the preparation of the public mind for a complete reformation of the order of things that prevailed in Russia, and for the impending change to the free, European political institutions.

The fiery Tolstoy, still scenting the gunpowder of the Sevastopol guns, obsessed by innumerable questions that had accumulated within him, and feeling almost a physical need to understand the problem of life, burst like a storm into this literary kingdom of the *Sovremennik.*

Politics held no interest for him. In the Russian social vortex of that day he was preoccupied with his unusually complex inner life. In the Caucasus, in Turkey, in Sevastopol, he had put himself through intensive tests. Drawn by the problems of war and death, as if they were the mystery of the sphinx, he had explored them eagerly. He had been anxious to experience all manner of dangers; and when, after a struggle with sensuousness, his powerful and passionate nature had broken through to excesses, he had frequently abandoned himself to the gambling spirit of the times, facing financial ruin across the card table. He had a craving for glory, but, unlike Turgenev, he never thought of adjusting himself to the tastes of the public. Forcefully and stormily he followed his own path, conquering the crowds with his originality. He hated everything conventional, everything fashionable, everything "epidemic." He wanted to explore with his own mind, and to entice humanity to follow him on the road indicated by his imaginative genius.

Tolstoy's broad, homely face, with its thick lips, was enlivened by his light-gray, deep-set, kind, expressive eyes. At heart he was a kind and simple man. Among unassuming people he was so unassuming, so natural, and so playful, that his presence usually stimulated everybody. In the minds of his fellow officers he always remained a gay, witty companion, a splendid horseman, and a man of uncommon physical strength. He won children over with a few words. Without the slightest conscious effort he knew how to entertain them and how to make them like him. His cousin, who occupied an important position at the imperial court, often told of Tolstoy's pranks, which brought disorder and general chaos into her well-regulated court life.

But, according to the naïve observations of a lady among his contemporaries, Tolstoy carried within himself several different natures, and he could be transformed into a totally unrecognizable person.

In the *Sovremennik* literary circle he very soon took the offensive. He was annoyed by their ways: their insincerity, their constant chase after fashionable democratic ideas, their adulation of Western authorities.

In Petersburg Tolstoy led a stormy, irregular life, and he not only made no effort to conceal his adventures, but openly boasted about them. At the same time the painful processes of self-analysis, of remorse, of self-improvement, and of a search for truth in morals, religion, and pure art were taking place within him. He could not go to the fashionable authors of the day with these delicate problems. He was seeking friendship— intimate personal companionship. Though they valued Tolstoy's talent and admired his creative genius, Turgenev and the other writers for the *Sovremennik* attempted to keep on a superficial, social footing with him. Tolstoy's sudden conclusions, his fight against everything conventional, and his paradoxes made them even more cautious. The danger of an unexpected and destructive explosion was ever present.

At one of the *Sovremennik* literary dinners a minor disagreement had taken place. Tolstoy had been warned that in that particular circle George Sand was greatly admired. The hostess (the wife of the publisher of the *Sovremennik*) liked to dream about the "rights of the heart" and "free love." During dinner the conversation turned to George Sand's latest novels. Tolstoy made no effort to restrain himself. He said, so that everyone present could hear him, that if women such as George Sand pictured existed, they should be pilloried and dragged through the streets as an example to the mob.

On one occasion the family of a famous sculptor was listening to a reading of the suppressed, but nevertheless fashionable, articles by the famous *émigré*, Herzen. In his later years, Tolstoy acquired a great respect for Herzen's opinions, but he felt differently in 1856. A witness relates that Count Tolstoy "entered the sitting room, while the reading was in progress. He stood quietly behind the chair of the man who was reading and waited until he had finished. Then, at first calmly and later with growing animation, he attacked Herzen and the widespread fad for his works." He spoke so sincerely and so convincingly that at least one family forever lost its taste for suppressed pamphlets.

Tolstoy's attacks on Shakespeare were the talk of the day among the Petersburg literati, who were all worshipers of the British genius.

These were only isolated instances. Soon Tolstoy took an open and obvious stand of "opposition to everything conventional in the realm of reasoning." No matter whose opinion was quoted, he felt the urge to take the opposite side, and a battle of words was under way. Watching him as he listened to the other man, seeing the penetrating look of his deep-set gray eyes and the ironical expression on his lips, one could easily surmise that he was not searching for a logical argument, but for something that would confuse his opponent and take him by surprise.

The disagreements with Turgenev became more frequent. Soon Tolstoy moved to an apartment of his own; but even after that, whenever they met, they engaged in warm, typically Russian arguments, which at times were likely to reach a dramatic climax. On one such occasion, Tolstoy, quivering with rage, said, "I will not permit him to do anything to spite me! He is walking in front of me right now, rolling his democratic hips—just to aggravate me!"

He almost fought a duel with Longinov, one of the group of writers living in Petersburg. One evening a number of people were playing cards in Nekrasov's home. A servant brought a letter from Longinov. Nekrasov, busy with the cards, asked Tolstoy to open the letter and read it aloud. Among other matters in his letter, Longinov—without mincing words—criticized Tolstoy's political backwardness and his reactionary opinions. Tolstoy made no comment, but that night, when he returned home, he wrote and sent a note to Longinov, challenging him to a duel.

Turgenev's opinion was that Tolstoy seldom believed that anyone was sincere. Every expression of emotion seemed artificial to him, and whenever he thought that a man talking to him was not sincere, he had the habit of fixing him with his unusually piercing eyes.

In his diary (September 10, 1852) Tolstoy confessed, "When talking, I involuntarily say with my eyes things that no one wants to hear, and which make me feel ashamed of myself."

3

Perhaps revolt against everything conventional was Tolstoy's most characteristic trait. It began when he was still in diapers. Tolstoy's earliest recollections belong to an unusually early age. Wrapped in blankets, he was lying in a semidarkness, crying at the top of his voice. His one desire was to be freed of the wrappings. Two worried heads were bent over him; they sympathized, but they made no move to help him. "They think that it is necessary to keep me wrapped, but I know that it is not. I wish to prove it to them, and I let out screams, which disgust me, but which I cannot hold back. . . . I want freedom, which cannot hurt anyone, and I, who need strength, am weak, while they are strong."

The philosopher in diapers "knows" better than the two grown people who love him, "knows" that it is unnecessary to wrap him, and he protests with all the means at his command.

Many stories of his early years have been preserved by Tolstoy's family. All of them give a picture of an animated, kind-hearted, remarkably sensitive boy, but at the same time they constantly refer to altogether unexpected outbursts with which the child wished to impress the grownups and which indicate his desire to do "the unusual."

His later life was full of humorous and tragic instances of his "struggle against prejudices."

Here is a story told by Count Nicholas, Tolstoy's elder brother, and recorded by Fet in 1858:

"Lev is intently seeking ways for a closer association with the life of the village and with the management of the estate, of which, like all of us, he so far has only a superficial knowledge. I have no notion what the results will be. Lev wants to do everything simultaneously, without sacrificing anything, not even his gymnastics. He has installed parallel bars under the windows of his room. Naturally, if one puts aside the prejudices against which he is always struggling, he is right. Gymnastics should not interfere with the management of the estate. But the overseer is of a different opinion. He says, 'I come to the master to get his orders, and I find him in a red jacket, swinging upside down from a bar by one leg, his moist hair dangling, his face a dark purple. I don't know what to do: to ask for orders, or to stand and watch the show.' "

During the winter of 1858, he went bear hunting. Usually the hunters were assigned places in a broken line, and were given time to trample the snow around them, so that they would have a certain freedom of movement. Everyone observed this precaution, but Tolstoy said, "Nonsense! I came here to shoot bears, and not to compete with them in digging snow." Obstinately, he stood in snow to his waist, his reserve gun leaning against a tree. Suddenly a large female bear appeared before him. He shot once and missed; he shot a second time, the bullet was stopped by her teeth and the wounded animal attacked him. He could not get out of her way in the deep snow. The bear trampled and clawed him, and only a lucky chance saved his life.

This proud determination to choose his own path, to depend entirely on his own resources, and not to recognize any traditions or authority, were a part of Tolstoy's nature. The element of discipline had never played a part in his upbringing. He lost his mother when he was two, and his father when he was nine years old. He grew up among women who loved him dearly, but who had no exceptional qualities and little influence over him. He was never subjected to school discipline.

He was prepared for a university in his home. Teachers came to give him lessons and tutors supervised his conduct. After he was admitted to the University of Kazan, Tolstoy was expected to attend the lectures, hand in his work, and pass examinations. But even these duties seemed unbearable to him, and he left during his second year. Actually he educated himself, and that was one of the reasons why he was accustomed to depend only on himself. The required subjects were a matter of supreme indifference to him, and he was always a poor student. From his earliest years he read a great deal, and philosophized even more. Even as a child and as a boy, he persisted in trying to solve the basic questions of human existence. When he was sixteen, he discarded religion and, instead of a cross, wore around his neck a medallion with a portrait of Jean Jacques Rousseau, whom he worshiped. He wrote philosophic treatises while he was still a child, and when his elders or his playmates saw his notebooks, they could not believe that Lev dwelt on such serious subjects. His busy mind was occupied with problems of moral self-training and self-improvement. Later he wrote, "Now, thinking of those days, I can clearly see that my faith—the only thing besides animal instincts that guided my life—my only faith was faith in self-improvement. But what this self-improvement was or what was its purpose, I could not explain. I tried to improve myself mentally: I learned everything I could, everything that

I saw in the course of my daily life; I tried to improve my will: I made rules that I forced myself to follow; I tried to improve my body through various physical exercises that required strength and speed, and through various privations taught my body to be patient and enduring. All this I considered self-improvement. Naturally, at the bottom of this, was a desire for moral improvement, that is, a desire to appear better not before myself, or before God, but a desire to appear better before other people. Very soon this desire to appear better before other people changed to a desire to be stronger than other people, to be better known, to be more important, and more wealthy."

The examples he had before him did not always encourage him toward moral improvement. On another occasion he said, "I was never taught any moral principles—none whatever—and all around me people drank, smoked, led immoral lives (most frequently led immoral lives), beat other men and made them work. I did many wicked things without realizing it, simply because I was imitating my elders."

Not all the temptations came from outside. It is hard to imagine an individual in whom the voice of nature and the craving for personal happiness spoke louder. At the same time, the longing for the good, the moral—for self-improvement—was very strong in him. Tolstoy could not have any personal happiness without satisfying this organic need. The two sides of his complex nature—his personal desires in the narrow sense and his longing for the general good—were in a constant state of conflict. Very few people have had to face as many temptations. His path toward "the good" was blocked not only by a passionate and physically strong nature but also by an unusually flexible, paradoxical mind, which, with remarkable virtuosity, always seconded his deep longing for personal happiness. His personal needs constantly made him ascribe new attributes to his general understanding of "the good." At the same time his make-up showed not the slightest trace of insincerity, which he detested in himself and in others.

4

Tolstoy left the university when he was nineteen, and went to live in the country. He believed that, within two years, he could easily prepare himself for the final examinations. Besides, he was attracted by the opportunity to help and guide the peasants of the village of Yasnaya Polyana, his share of the family estate, which had been divided among the brothers. He considered it his unquestionable and sacred duty to care for the seven hundred people for whom he felt responsible to God.

Planning the happiness of the peasants proved to be not such an easy task. Later he described his disappointments in a story, *The Landlord's Morning.* The attempt to manage his estate was also not a success, and Tolstoy soon began to feel that it was a heavy burden on him.

In the autumn of 1847 he gave up the village life, and plunged wholeheartedly into the urban temptations of Moscow. He led a life typical of the "gilded youth" of the period: he frequently appeared at social gatherings, he danced and flirted, he took up fencing and gymnastics, he rode horseback in a manège, he took part in wild debauches, often visited the gypsies (whose singing he loved), and lost large sums gambling. . . . A life of this kind could not satisfy Tolstoy. He felt remorseful, confessed his sins in his diary, repented, and full of good intentions, went back to the country. But very soon he again appeared in Moscow and surrendered to passions and temptations. At times he would decide that "one cannot live on reasoning and philosophy, but that one must lead a constructive life—one must be practical." On one such occasion he applied for a position in one of the state offices in Tula. On another similar occasion he went to Petersburg to pass his final university examinations, but unexpectedly —even for him—gave up the examinations and took every possible step to get an appointment as a cadet in one of the exclusive guard regiments, so that he could take part in the Hungarian campaign. Having firmly resolved to remain in Petersburg "forever," he suddenly left for Yasnaya Polyana, because the spring in the country beckoned to him. On one occasion when he was in a practical frame of mind, he even decided to engage in a commercial enterprise; he secured a mail contract in Tula from the government, but fortunately he sold it before he lost too much money. Once, seeing off his sister's fiancé, he jumped into the carriage when it was already in motion, and the only reason he did not make the journey to Siberia was because he had left his hat at home.

Not all his escapades ended well. His small fortune was dwindling rapidly. Sometimes he did not have enough money to pay his gambling debts. In the spring of 1848, in a characteristic letter to his brother, Count Sergei, he wrote, "Sooner or later I had to pay for my freedom (I had no one to whip me—that was my biggest trouble) and for my philosophy, and now the day of reckoning is here. Please do something to get me out of the false and disgusting situation in which I find myself at present—without a cent, and owing money to everyone."

The first stormy period of his life came to an end on April 20, 1851. He reached a sudden decision: "to exile myself to the Caucasus, so I can escape my debts, and, more than anything else, my habits." He left with his elder brother, Count Nicholas, who was serving in the artillery and who was going back from a leave.

Tolstoy spent almost two and a half years in the Caucasus (1851–54). His life there he described in *The Invaders, The Wood-cutting Expedition, An Old Acquaintance, Recollections of a Marker,* and especially vividly in *The Cossacks.* About six months after his arrival he enlisted as a cadet in the artillery, saw action against the mountain tribesmen, and was frequently exposed to danger. But even in the Caucasus he could not rid himself of the "habits" that he had tried to leave behind him in Moscow. The association with his fellow officers virtually forced him to take part in their drinking and gambling. His passion for gambling came to the fore, and he often lost sums of money that he could obtain only with the utmost difficulty. While he was living in Tiflis, Tolstoy became enthusiastic about billiards. He made up his mind to beat—at any cost—a famous local marker, played a thousand games against him, and lost almost his entire fortune.

In January, 1854, he passed his examinations, was given leave, and went home to receive his commission. The war with Turkey had begun. Tolstoy wanted to see action; by using his family connections he secured an assignment to the Army of the Danube, and took part in the siege of the Turkish fortress of Silistra. When England and France entered the war, he persisted in asking for an assignment to Sevastopol, chiefly—as he wrote to his brother Sergei—out of a feeling of "patriotism." Tolstoy remained in Sevastopol for a year (November, 1854, to November, 1855). Part of the time he spent in the outlying districts, and part of the time in most dangerous posts. On two occasions, as a volunteer, he took part in sorties. On the whole, Tolstoy proved to be a good officer. Among the various forms of "glory" he was seeking at the time, was the "glory of service rendered for the good of one's country." Most of his army career was spent in staff assignments, in which he performed his duties exceptionally well. But he never tried to avoid service in the line. On the contrary, he sought danger. While living under terrible conditions and freezing in the trenches, he wrote a long report advocating the formation of special mortar batteries and the general reorganization of artillery. Thoughts about the men entrusted to his care were always uppermost in his mind. In his diaries he accused himself of haughtiness, of irritability, and of inability to get along with people, but his fellow officers seemed to retain throughout their lives extremely pleasant recollections of their associations with him during the war. Among the generally prevalent laxity in the handling of government money, he preached to his fellow officers the need of returning to the treasury anything they had saved from the regulation allowance for the upkeep of their horses.

However, glory awaited him in a different field. The officially sanctioned inactivity, the company of his fellow officers, their interests and habits, which affected his impressionable nature, depressed him. He always towered above his surroundings, but his official status was not enviable. At twenty-six he was a second lieutenant, and every youngster newly graduated from the military academies either outranked him or was his equal. Besides, in the eyes of his superiors he had been compromised by participating in the composition of the "Sevastopol Songs." A group of Sevastopol officers were in the habit of gathering around a piano; one would play, while the others—to the tunes of Russian folk songs—would compose verses ridiculing the generals and their military failures. All of these songs were ascribed to Tolstoy, and the talk in the higher military circles in Petersburg was that he had not only composed them but even taught his soldiers to sing them.

The thought of leaving the army had occurred to him on several occasions while he was still in the Caucasus and in Sevastopol. After he arrived in Petersburg, he made the decision, though his resignation could not be accepted until the war was over. In the capital he was assigned to the artillery section of the Ministry of War, and he immediately asked for and received an eleven-months' leave, which he spent in Moscow, in Petersburg, and in the country. Toward the end of 1856 he at last discarded the uniform and soon afterward left for a journey abroad. He spent six stormy months in Paris and Switzerland.

The next five years of Tolstoy's life, as usual, seethed with a variety of activities. His brilliant literary achievements already pointed to his lifetime work. But his wholehearted nature could not be satisfied with the role of a mere writer of stories and novels. Tolstoy wanted and sought a fuller life. Among other things, the village life and his country estate once again appealed to him. But at Yasnaya Polyana he was confronted with serfdom, to which he could never adjust himself. Humanitarian ideas, which filled the minds of the liberals and which were the fashionable ideas of his day, had no effect on him. He tried to work for the well-being of his "subjects," as he called his peasants, and encountered bitter disappointments. He had nothing in common with them, not even a common language. He could not even get the peasants to believe in him. He had to accept the destitute, downtrodden village, or else to discard from his conscience the responsibility for the fate of the "subjects." Besides, during the transition stage, while the peasants were impatiently awaiting their emancipation, the management of the estate according to the old methods was a difficult problem. Tolstoy had no faith in governmental reform. He at once decided to free his peasants on his own, and to divide the land between them in a way that would not affect his welfare too adversely. He pushed this matter energetically in Petersburg circles, and he finally found a solution acceptable to the Treasury, which held a twenty-thousand-ruble mortgage on the estate. But all his efforts were defeated by the obstinate refusal of the peasants, who were daydreaming about the coronation of Alexander II and the day when they should receive the land belonging to the great land-owners absolutely free. This failure cooled Tolstoy's ardor for country life, but his interest in agriculture—about which he knew very little—reasserted itself from time to time. With good-natured irony his elder brother said, "The way Yufan, the laborer, sticks out his elbows when he plows appeals to Lev. At once Yufan becomes to him a symbol of village strength, something of a folklore knight. So Lev takes a plow, sticks out his elbows, and proceeds to 'Yufanize.'" Tolstoy always had a romantic conception of agriculture, but at times, in the midst of his enthusiasm for it, he experienced an unbearable feeling of disgust, and escaped to the city, back to literature, society, and the study of music. On one such occasion he wrote in his diary, "Farming is crushing me with its reeking weight."

He loved music passionately, and in his younger years had serious aspirations in that field. He not only worked diligently at the piano but also studied the theory of music and even tried to compose. These efforts failed to make him a musician, but music always retained its hold on him.

The suddenness with which he frequently changed his mind surprised everybody. Once after he had planted a number of young trees on his estate, he suddenly decided that the future happiness of Russia depended on reforestation on a national scale. He at once worked out an elaborate reforestation project, took it to Petersburg, and tried everything in his power to make the government undertake it. It is hardly necessary to say that these efforts were unsuccessful. When, in the midst of an argument, Turgenev asked him what he considered his real calling in life, Tolstoy very positively, and with great self-assurance, answered, "I am a forester." In describing this episode to his friends, Turgenev wrote, "I am afraid that he may dislocate the backbone of his talent by this constant changing about."

When Tolstoy was abroad in 1857, he read some stories of village life by Berthold Auerbach, and he at once decided to devote his life to teaching peasants. A small school already existed in Yasnaya Polyana, founded by Tolstoy in the late forties. But the teaching was done by an old serf who had constantly to be warned against whipping the children "for their own good." Whenever Tolstoy was at the school, he created an atmosphere of life, noisy gaiety, and tenderness. He loved children and liked to play with them. When he was away, the school, in the hands of the old serf, rapidly went down.

In July, 1857, Tolstoy wrote in his diary, ". . . and most important of all: clearly and forcibly the thought came to me to open a school for the entire county, and to engage in a number of other activities in the same field." Only two years later, in the fall of 1859, he came close to realizing his dreams. With the same passion with which he did everything, he gave himself to teaching. Almost to the exclusion of all other interests, he gave three years of his life to the peasant children. His work had nothing in common with the standard, well-regulated school systems. Tolstoy wrote that he had a "passionate affection" for his school. Under his guidance, other young people who helped him in his work developed a similar "passionate affection." As usual, he began by discarding all existing traditions, and by refusing to follow any method of teaching already in use. First, he must fathom the mind of the peasant child, and by doing away with punishments, let his pupils teach him the art of teaching. In his school the pupils were free to choose their own subjects, and to take as much work as they desired. The teacher considered it his duty to assist the children in their search for knowledge by adjusting his method of approach to the individual child, and by finding the best way of proffering assistance in each case. These free Tolstoy schools, without programs, without punishments, without rules, without forcing the will of the child, were remarkably successful. The children spent entire days at their studies and were reluctant to leave the schoolhouses.

Fifty years later, Basil Morosov, one of the Yasnaya Polyana peasants, said, "Hours passed by like minutes. If life were always as gay, no one would ever notice it go by. . . . In our pleasures, in our gaiety, in our rapid progress, we soon became as thick as thieves with the Count. . . . We were unhappy without the Count, and the Count was unhappy without us. We were inseparable, and only night drew us apart. We spent the day in school, and in the evenings we played games, or sat on his porch until midnight. He told us stories: stories about the war, about his aunt who had been murdered in Moscow by her cook, about hunting, about the bear that almost killed him, and he showed us the scar from the bear's claws above his eye. There was no end to our conversations. We told him a lot of things: about sorcerers, about forest devils. . . . He told us horrible and funny fairy tales, and he sang songs, making up words as he went along. The Count always liked to joke and never missed an opportunity to laugh or to say something funny. He always had nicknames for all of us."

With such a teacher the schoolwork naturally progressed remarkably well. However, in building his new, individual methods of teaching, Tolstoy tried to familiarize himself, as far as he could, with the current theories of education. He read a great many books on education, especially by German authors, and when he went abroad again in 1860–61, he took every opportunity to study the various school systems in Germany and in France. In his biography of Tolstoy, Raphael Lowenfeld has given a detailed description of Tolstoy's studies in Germany and his meetings and conversations with the leading educators and scientists of the day.

But neither the foreign nor the Russian schools, nor the theories of the leading educators, could satisfy Tolstoy. Other people's thoughts and opinions on any subject served only as a starting point for the independent workings of his mind. In almost every instance the material was discarded. He was never satisfied to say, "No"; he always had to add, "No, it's impossible." He had a habit of saying, "Not only has it never been that way, it never could have been." He settled in every one of his thoughts as if it were a fortress, and no efforts of his adversaries could dislodge him from the position he occupied. As time went on, new ideas appeared. Ideas just as arrogant, just as self-confident, just as final—and then, without a struggle, the old ideas gave up the stronghold to the newcomers and disappeared without leaving a trace.

The unreserved enthusiasm of Tolstoy's nature can be appreciated in his article, "Should We Teach the Peasant Children, or Should the Peasant Children Teach Us?" Describing a lesson period during which he had taught the children composition, he wrote, "For a long time I could not account for what I had experienced. . . . On the following day I could not believe my experiences of the day before. It seemed so strange to me that an eleven-year-old peasant boy, barely able to read, should display a conscious artistic power never reached even by Goethe at his indescribable height of development. It seemed to be so puzzling and so insulting to me, that I, the author of *Childhood*, which met with a certain amount of success and which brought recognition of my artistic talent by the intelligent Russian public, was not only unable to guide and help an eleven-year-old boy's artistic sense, but that I was barely able to follow and understand him, and then only during lucky moments when I was stimulated by irritation."

This remarkable article appeared in *Yasnaya Polyana*, a magazine for teachers, edited by Tolstoy during the year 1862. In the pages of this modest publication he shared with the public his experiences as a teacher and, as usual, discussed the basic problems of human existence.

⌈On February 19, 1861, the Russian peasants were emancipated. The next step was to supply them with land, which had to be apportioned among them out of the estates of their former owners. This work required the services of qualified arbitrators who could adjust matters equitably between the landowners and the peasants. To fill this need the office of "public arbitrator" was created, who during the transitional period was also to perform the duties of a circuit judge. Tolstoy was abroad. The Governor of Tula decided to enlist his services. The government insisted upon its choice, over the unanimous opposition of the local landowners, who were suspicious of Tolstoy's love of the peasants; and Tolstoy accepted the appointment, although fully aware of the opposition. He wrote, "My conscience would not let me refuse the appointment because of the horrible, boorish, and cruel nobility, who promised to eat me alive if I became an arbitrator."

He began the work in May, 1861, and for almost a year continued a desperate struggle to defend the interests of the peasants against the landowners.

His decisions were usually reversed by the county council of arbitrators. He received many threatening letters: he was to be beaten or shot in a duel. Complaints against him poured into the capital.⌋

Tolstoy's sanguine nature was well suited to these stormy activities.

To his friend and relative, Countess Alexandra Tolstoy, a lady in waiting at the imperial court, he wrote during the early part of this period (October, 1857), "Constant worry, work, struggle, privations—these are all necessary conditions, from which, even for a few seconds, no one should dare think of escaping. Only honest work, worry, and struggle—based on love—make for true happiness. And what is happiness, except a stupid word?—goodness, and not happiness. Dishonest worry,

based on love for oneself, is a misfortune. . . . It seems strange
that I thought, and you still, I believe, think, that one can create
a happy and honest world in which one can live quietly, without
making mistakes, without regrets, without complications, and
in which one can serenely, neatly, deliberately do only good
things. It's funny! It's impossible! It's just as impossible as remaining healthy without moving, without exercising. . . . To
live honestly it is necessary to yearn, to get entangled, to fight,
to make mistakes, to begin things and to drop them, then begin
and drop them again, and constantly to struggle and deprive
onself. Serenity is nothing more than cowardice of the soul. That
is why the bad side of our souls seeks peace, without realizing
that its achievement means the loss of everything beautiful
within us—loss of that which is not of human creation and
comes from above."

Reading this letter over when he was eighty, Tolstoy said that
he could not think of any changes in the philosophy of life it
expressed. But in 1862 he was tired.

His country estate was not thriving. His literary fame was on
the down grade, though he had published within four years
(1856–59) a series of remarkable stories. In 1856: *Sevastopol in
August, Lost in the Steppe, Two Hussars, The Landlord's Morning, An Old Acquaintance.* In 1857: *Youth, Lucerne.* In 1858:
Albert. In 1859: *Three Deaths,* and a novel, *Family Happiness.*
These masterpieces were received with indifference. Russian society was groaning with the pangs of rebirth. The public and the
critics demanded sociological themes of a sensational character.
Pure art, unrelated to the events of the day, went unnoticed.
Extremely sensitive to his diminishing reputation, Tolstoy
stopped publishing his stories, and in response to the remon-
strances of his friends answered that he had decided to become
a writer for his own pleasure.

Tolstoy found his association with the peasant children extremely pleasant, but he expected too much from his school.
Later he wrote, "I told myself that in certain cases progress follows an irregular path, and that we have to approach primitive

people as naturally as we can, helping them to follow the particular path of progress that they have chosen themselves." The "primitive people" delighted in their association with the genius, and repaid his thoughtful solicitude with tender love. Unfortunately they could not give him the answer he was seeking. The true path of human progress remained as much of a mystery to Tolstoy as it was to the peasant children.

The magazine in which he searchingly and independently considered the basic problems of education had a cold reception, entirely lacking in understanding. No one argued with Tolstoy, but then almost no one took an interest in his new ideas in the field of education. Many of these ideas, however, bore the trace of genius, and fifty years later attracted the attention of leading American and Russian educators. In the early sixties most people considered his magazine an amateur gentleman's fancy. *Yasnaya Polyana* had few subscribers, lasted only a year, and cost Tolstoy three thousand rubles.

Because of continuously growing opposition on the part of the landowners, his position as arbitrator became impossible, especially as the way in which he handled formalities and routine work (to which he paid little attention) gave just grounds for complaints.

In addition to all these discouragements fate, during this period, sent Tolstoy two other heavy trials.

On September 20, 1860, Count Nicholas Tolstoy died of tuberculosis in the south of France. From hour to hour for a month, Lev had watched his brother's life being painfully extinguished. He "loved and respected him above anyone in the world. . . . This clever, kind, serious man fell sick while he was still young, suffered over a year, and died a painful death, without being able to comprehend why he had lived, still less why he had to die. No theories could give a satisfactory answer to these questions to me, or to him during the slow and painful approach of death." Tolstoy refused to believe in the eternal life of the individual, and for him Count Nicholas disappeared forever, "like a piece of wood that has been burned."

Lev Tolstoy was sharply, persistently, painfully confronted by the problem of death. Everything around him seemed to fade. "What is the purpose of anything, if tomorrow will bring the pains of death with all its disgusting lies and self-deceptions, and leading into nothingness, into a zero for oneself? . . ." His appetite for life had left him. Even his school at Yasnaya Polyana was temporarily forgotten. He had no desire to go home.

He wrote, "What difference does it make where I spend the rest of my life? I am living here, and I may as well stay here." He had no intention of writing; he had become too absorbed in his dark and sad thoughts.

"If he could not find anything to support him, what can I hope for? I have even less to go on. . . ."

Count Nicholas Tolstoy had been an exceptionally charming man: kind, with a touch of irony, according to his friends he exemplified during his life everything that Lev Tolstoy preached in his later years. There was no desire for fame, no vanity in Nicholas Tolstoy; and though he had inherited from his mother a remarkable talent for storytelling, he almost never attempted to write and limited himself to giving literary advice to his younger brother. Turgenev insisted that Nicholas Tolstoy "lacked only a few of the attributes that make a man a great writer."

From his early youth Nicholas Tolstoy had exercised a great deal of influence on his brother Lev. This influence can be described as Christian, or, perhaps more correctly, as humane. While he was still a child, he enticed his brothers into a realm of fantastic thoughts, in which a prominent part was played by the "brotherhood of ants, lovingly hugging one another," and by the famous green stick on which was written "the great mystery of how to arrange things so that people would never know misfortune, would never quarrel or be angry, and would be happy constantly."

For Tolstoy the kind, delicate, tender personality of his brilliant elder brother was the embodiment of "good," of Christian virtue, of self-sacrifice. . . . That is why Count Nicholas's untimely and painful death was such a heavy blow to him.

A few months later, however, Tolstoy's interests were making themselves felt again. First he became interested in working with the children of his sister, who was also living in the south of France. He again began to write articles on public education for future publication. This led him to a further study of the school systems of France, England, and Germany. At last he decided to go home to Yasnaya Polyana, where his school and new troubles in connection with his work as arbitrator awaited him. The wound was gradually healing. Temporarily the vision of death retreated into his subconscious. But his enjoyment of life had suffered its first blow, and he felt the results later.

The second trial, though a less painful one, was his final quarrel with Turgenev.

Their relations had continued to be rather indefinite and uncertain. They had met abroad in 1857, they had spent many days together, but both seemed reluctant to pass a certain point in their friendship. In his diaries Tolstoy at times pitied Turgenev, at others recorded pleasant days he had spent in his company, and on occasion described his great indignation with him. In addition to holding differing opinions and belonging to diametrically opposed schools of thought, they were estranged by another factor. Countess Mary Tolstoy, Lev's sister, was unhappy in her marriage. In 1857 she and her husband finally separated. Turgenev, who was an old friend though he was on very intimate terms with Mme Viardot, could not resist the pleasure of a flirtation with the clever Countess, who greatly valued his companionship. This relationship frightened Tolstoy, and he very emphatically disapproved of it.

Nevertheless, the two writers were drawn to each other. In the spring of 1861 Turgenev was living in Spaskoye, his country estate in the Province of Orel, where he was putting the finishing touches on his best novel, *Fathers and Sons*. Tolstoy stopped by Turgenev's home, so that they could go to visit their mutual friend Fet together. Their meeting in Spaskoye was very cordial.

At dinner Turgenev, with a certain show of emotion, spoke of his newly finished novel. Tolstoy expressed his desire to read the manuscript. After dinner the host carefully set the stage in the living room: all the flies were killed, and a small table with the manuscript, smoking paraphernalia, and drinks was moved close to a huge divan. When everything was ready, Turgenev tiptoed out of the room and carefully closed the door behind him, so that nothing should disturb his guest.

In the absolute stillness Tolstoy began to read. Soon his eyes became heavy and, before he knew it, he was dozing.

Suddenly something gave him a jolt. He awoke in time to see Turgenev's back as he was walking out of the room.

The novel was never mentioned again.

Outwardly on the best of terms, they arrived at Fet's house. The next morning over the breakfast table the final curtain fell on their friendship.

Turgenev was speaking about the education of his daughter. Tolstoy made several critical remarks.

His nostrils quivering, Turgenev exclaimed, "I will ask you not to talk about it in this manner!"

"Why shouldn't I express my convictions?"

Turgenev's face turned white and he shouted, "If you say another word, I will slap your face!"

Clutching his head in his hands, and swaying from side to side, Turgenev walked quickly out of the room. When he had a grip on himself, he returned and apologized to his hostess.

Tolstoy left immediately, without saying a word; but from the next relay station he wrote Turgenev a letter demanding a formal apology or, in default of that, challenging him to a duel. In this letter he expressed his intention not to have a conventional duel with seconds, doctors, and champagne. He suggested that Turgenev should meet him at the edge of the forest with a loaded shotgun, so that they could have a "real" duel without witnesses.

Turgenev apologized, but they remained estranged for seventeen years.

All these bitter disappointments finally told on Tolstoy's health. In the summer of 1861 he began coughing blood. The threat of tuberculosis and death was on him. The doctors prescribed a complete rest in the Tartar steppes and a diet of horse milk. It was not until the following year that Tolstoy followed their advice. He resigned from his position as arbitrator, discontinued the publication of his magazine, gave the management of his school over to his assistants, and, taking with him two of his pet pupils from among the peasant boys, started out for the Province of Samara.

5

Was Tolstoy in the habit of falling in love? In 1856 he wrote, "I am not speaking of the love of a young man for a young woman. On the contrary, I am afraid of that kind of attachment. Unfortunately, never in my life have I seen a trace of truth in this type of love—nothing but lies, in which sensuality, marital relations, money, desire to be independent and to be settled, obscured the sentiment itself to a point where it was impossible to analyze it."

These are the words of Nicholas Irtenyev in *Youth*. In *Childhood* the same character tells of his love for little Sonya Valakhin, and in *Youth* of the first stages of his attraction for Princess Neklyudov. Tolstoy has left evidence that these pictures were taken from real life. In his childhood he was very much attracted by little Sonya Koloshin, and in his youth by Alexandra Dyakov, a sister of one of his friends at the university. In 1858 and 1859, after Alexandra Dyakov had married a "charming man," Prince Andrew Obolensky, he met her again in Moscow. The old emotion flared up, stronger than ever, but the Princess, realizing the danger of an intimate friendship with such a fascinating man, moved to Petersburg, taking her children.

Tolstoy had several flirtations while he was studying in Kazan. He believed that he was attracted most by Zinaida Molostvov. He met that attractive and gifted girl again in 1851, when he and his brother were on their way to the Caucasus, and he devoted a tender page to her in his diary. A strong feeling in both seemed to be in the making, but circumstances prevented its further development.

In the Caucasus Tolstoy fell in love with a Cossack girl. Though the plot of *The Cossacks* describes the actual experiences of another person, according to the author, the love of Dmitri Olenin for Mariana is based on Tolstoy's own feelings for the young Cossack girl.

Tolstoy had no more constant and cherished dream than the dream of a family, marriage, and children of his own. His letters and diaries refer to it constantly, but it was difficult for him to find a suitable life companion. He demanded too much intellect, sincerity, and beauty from the girls he met. The wife he sought must be a strong and healthy mother for his children, able to nurse and care for them herself. She must look at the world through her husband's eyes and be his constant companion. Though she must possess social graces, she must be willing to forget society, settle with her husband in the country, and devote her entire life to her family.

With his unusual insight into human nature, only an irresistible passion could have made him believe that he had at last found the embodiment of his ideals.

As the years passed, he consciously became willing to make allowances. His relations with Valeria Arsenyev can be explained in this light. The girl was an orphan and lived with her younger sister and their devoted governess in Sudakovo, the family country estate, only five miles from Yasnaya Polyana. The Tolstoy family had known Valeria Arsenyev's parents well. The girls visited in Yasnaya Polyana. In 1856 Lev Tolstoy frequently visited Sudakovo. The governess, Mlle Vergani, concocted a plot for a match between Tolstoy and Valeria. Evidently the girl liked the idea. True, she was inclined to dream of clothes, social pleasures, and brilliant uniforms, but Count Tolstoy seemed a desirable match. Toward the end of October Lev Tolstoy could not resist the temptation to show Valeria a page in his diary on which he had written, "I love her." From that time on, they were considered engaged, but Tolstoy could not make up his mind. He doubted, thought, cooled off, then experienced a stronger feeling than ever before, and finally decided to test their love by a separation for two months. His aunt, who looked forward to the marriage, said that, very unexpectedly, "he started out for Petersburg instead of for church." A long exchange of letters followed. At a distance Valeria Arsenyev seemed less appealing. Tolstoy confessed to himself that it was not so much a case of his love for her, as of his desire to awaken in her a love for him. He felt that his feeling was dying, and he decided to write to Sudakovo directly and straightforwardly. Valeria Arsenyev's relations, and even his own aunt, were very much provoked with him. But he had tested himself thoroughly and could not have done anything else. Fortunately for everyone concerned, Valeria married happily soon afterward and had a family of four children.

With the thought of marriage constantly uppermost in his mind, Tolstoy was greatly tempted during his stay in Switzerland in the spring and summer of 1857. There he met and for the first time became intimate with his distant relatives, Countesses Elizabeth and Alexandra Tolstoy. They both held official positions at the court of Grand Duchess Marie. Alexandra Tolstoy was very good-looking and had a beautiful singing voice, which she worked hard to develop. Her directness of manner, her sincerity, her warm heart, her perpetual yearning for moral self-exploration and self-improvement made her exceptionally appealing. She had a brilliant mind and at the same time was very religious in a strict, orthodox sense. The social poise and reserve she had acquired at court did not prevent her from appreciating the quality of her stormy cousin, who was always likely to do the unexpected. In the tender friendship that sprang up between them Tolstoy was inclined to use his paradoxical mind and his skepticism in religious matters as weapons of flirtation. He sincerely believed that his "dear granny," as he had nicknamed her, was head and shoulders above all women he had ever met. Later they became estranged over religious convictions, but even shortly before his death, after looking over his correspondence with Countess Alexandra, he said to his friends, "In my long and dark life my recollections of Alexandra are always a bright spot that is like a light glowing under a door at the end of a dark hall." In the poetical setting of a spring in Switzerland, on the shores of Lake Geneva, their friendship continued to grow, and it seemed as though real feeling would develop. But the Countess was eleven years Tolstoy's senior; he noticed the first lines on her sweet, animated face, and often in his diary he sadly exclaimed, "If she were only ten years younger! . . ." They never became more than friends.

In 1859, while he was interested in several young ladies in Moscow, he finally made up his mind to propose to Princess Lvov, but was refused. Much later his wife said that during those years he was very unattractive physically and that "his face was provoking, passionate, and restless." Other girls who knew him found that conversations with him were "interesting but trying." Apparently his exceptionally complex spiritual make-up and his uncanny insight were too much of a strain for them.

His young years were behind him. He was beginning to notice signs of approaching age, and he was almost ready to forget the dream of family happiness that he had dreamed so tenderly and so long.

Chapter Two

IN THE 1850's Moscow was still an overgrown village. People lived under primitive conditions, in a free and easy way. There were few strangers. No artificial barriers, such as those that separated the Petersburg social circles from the rest of humanity, existed in their lives. The middle and upper classes, consisting of the landed gentry and government officials of all ranks, mixed freely. Under such conditions even the unassuming family of Dr. Behrs was generally accepted in society. The doctor worked for the imperial court and occupied a comfortable government apartment in the Kremlin. He had horses and some ten servants. In addition to his salary, though he was never considered a medical light, he received a good income from his practice. He had enough to live comfortably but there was little left over. Andrew Behrs belonged to the Lutheran church and was of German descent. He received a commission as major general in the medical corps in 1864; in the early forties he had been ennobled in recognition of his services. In 1842, when he was thirty-four years old, he married Lyubov Islavin, who was then sixteen. The girl's family history is more interesting. On her mother's side she was the granddaughter of Count Zavadovsky, the famous favorite of Catherine the Great and of Alexander I. Zavadovsky's eldest daughter, Countess Sophia, married Prince Kozlovsky when she was still very young. Their marriage was a failure. They soon separated, and the young Countess fell in love with Alexander Islenyev, with whom she spent fifteen years of her life and to whom, when she died, she left six children—three boys and three girls. She had not succeeded in obtaining a divorce from Prince Kozlovsky, though Islenyev had used all the influence he had. Nor was he able to win recognition for the children, and they bore the name of Islavin. The family lived the year round in the village of Krasnoye, in the Province of Tula, about thirty-five miles from Yasnaya Polyana. Islenyev was a friend of Count Nicholas Tolstoy, the father of the great writer. Their families also were friendly and spent weeks visiting each other in Krasnoye and in Yasnaya Polyana. The story goes that the nine-year-old Tolstoy was attracted by the eleven-year-old Lyubov Islavin and in a jealous fit pushed the girl down the stairs, hurting her so that she was lame for some time. When Tolstoy decided to write *Childhood, Boyhood,* and *Youth,* he wrote about this family of friends, changing their name to Irtenyev, and later interweaving his own experiences and pictures of his own childhood days with the Islenyev family history.

Lyubov Behrs presented her husband with thirteen children, eight of whom lived. Three girls and one boy came a year apart, and then, at irregular intervals, four more boys appeared in the nursery. In 1862 the eldest daughter, Elizabeth, was nineteen; Sophia, eighteen; and Tatyana, sixteen. The girls were educated at home. In addition to the usual German and French governesses, teachers came to their home and taught them in their own classroom. They were brought up in the old traditional atmosphere; but times were unsettled, and young ladies could not be entirely isolated from the new and fashionable ideas. In her autobiography Sophia (then Countess Tolstoy) wrote, "Students from the university taught us Russian and the various branches of science. One of them tried to convert me to an extreme materialistic outlook. He brought books by Büchner and Feuerbach for me to read, and tried to convince me that there was no God and that religion was mere superstition that had outlived its usefulness. At first the simplicity of the atom theory, and the idea that the whole universe depended on their interrelation, appealed to me, but very soon I began to miss my Orthodox faith and the Church, to which I was devoted, and I forsook materialistic theories forever." Despite that, Turgenev's *Fathers and Sons,* which had just been published, made a great impression on the Behrs family, and the girls were even inclined to sympathize with the nihilist, Bazarov. The idea that they would have to earn their own living was impressed on them early. They had to teach their younger brothers, they had to sew, embroider, keep house, and prepare themselves for teachers' licenses. The relations between their parents were not by any means exemplary, but they were not bad enough to poison the children's lives. Dr. Behrs was good-natured, but he had a very uneven disposition, and his sudden fits of anger frequently disrupted the even tenor of life in the household. On the whole, the calm, reserved Lyubov Behrs, who knew how to handle her husband, held the reins.

About two years after Tolstoy married Sophia Behrs, he wrote her a letter in which he described her relatives to her: "There are the 'black' Behrses—Mrs. Behrs, you, Tatyana, and Peter; and there are the 'white' Behrses—all the others. In the 'black' Behrses the mind is asleep; they *can*, but they have no desire, and that's why they have tact and self-assurance, which is not always well timed. Their minds are asleep because they love too much, and also because the oldest of their clan, Mrs. Behrs, is not too well developed. The 'white' Behrses, on the other hand, have a longing for intellectual pursuits, but their minds are weak and shallow." As soon as this remarkably good characterization is grasped, the individual differences in the three sisters can be understood. The eldest, Elizabeth, was a tall, beautiful girl, with serious, classical features and very expressive eyes. She was cool, uncommunicative, calm, and displayed very little energy. She looked on daily housework with disdain. Small children, their food, and their diapers, bored and disgusted her. She always had a book in her hand, she studied a number of subjects—English among them—and she translated from German. She wrote passable articles, some of which were later published. The sense of duty that she cultivated made her frequently force herself to do favors for the people who surrounded her, but Tolstoy's opinion was that her manner was "awkward and unsympathetic." Father's pet—the youngest sister, nicknamed "the little devil"—was the opposite extreme. "The little devil" was the stormy petrel of the household. Tatyana Behrs knew how to arouse her eldest sister as well as her dignified mother. She very early showed promise as a beautiful contralto, and she devoted much time to the study of music. Her temperament was that of an artist—passionate, enthusiastic. She threw her entire being into everything she did. With a natural directness, she openly displayed her egoism and self-admiration. But at the same time she had a very warm heart, which was filled with love for her friends.

Sophia Behrs—or Sonya, as she was always called in the family—was a cross between her two sisters. She disliked her cold and methodical elder sister, and all through her life she had a close and warm relationship with the younger one. Quite late in life Tatyana wrote about her sister: "Sonya was a healthy, pink-cheeked girl with large, dark-brown eyes and dark braids. She was very lively, but she had a sentimental streak in her, which could instantly make her sad. Sonya never surrendered to the gaiety and happiness that filled her youth and the first years of her married life. She seemed to mistrust happiness, and she never learned how to accept and enjoy it. She always seemed to think that something would intrude, or that something was lacking to make her happiness complete. She retained this trait all through her life. She realized this, and in one of her letters to me wrote, 'The remarkable and enviable gift of enjoying everything and everybody is conspicuous in you. I, on the contrary, always find something sad in gaiety and happiness.' " Dr. Behrs was in the habit of saying, "Poor Sonya will never be entirely happy." She was the essence of femininity and she loved children. She often spent her time in the nursery playing with her little brothers. She amused them when they were sick—to entertain them she learned to play the harmonica; and she frequently helped her mother with the household duties. Even, early in life, she was inclined to be saving, not to say parsimonious. Though she had no special talents, she loved literature, painting, and music. From her eleventh year she systematically kept a diary and sometimes wrote stories. In her autobiography she wrote, "Tolstoy's *Childhood* and Dickens' *David Copperfield* made the greatest impression on me. When I finished reading *Copperfield*, I cried because I was sorry to part with the people who had become so dear to me."

A minor incident occurred in connection with Tolstoy's *Childhood*. Reading it, Sonya Behrs became so enthusiastic that she learned a number of passages by heart and copied them in her diary. Among them was the passage: "Will the freshness, the carefree spirit, the longing for love, and the strength of faith that one has in one's childhood ever return? What phase in life can be better than the one in which the two perfect qualities—innocent gaiety and a limitless longing for love—are the only motivating forces in life?" Elizabeth could not pass up this opportunity and wrote on the other side of the page in the diary, "Fool!" She despised it when "our sweet thing goes in for poetry and sentimentality." But being sentimental does not always mean being impractical. Obviously it did not in Sonya Behrs's case. She very early learned to appreciate the material things in life; she reached out for them, and she would not part with anything she had.

The desire to be liked and to be a success with men, the thirst for universal love and admiration were equally strong in the two younger sisters and added to their characters the trait that Tolstoy's friend, the poet Fet, described when he said, "Though they were very carefully supervised by their mother, and though the Behrs girls were irreproachably modest, they possessed that very attractive quality that the French mean when they say *du chien*." In the youngest of the sisters, this was, to a great extent, an outward reflection of a passionate nature. Sonya showed it in her innocent and clever way of flirting, with which she subconsciously tried to win a place in the sun. In the presence of men the girls' manners lacked conventional coyness—that stock in trade of provincial young ladies of the time. On the contrary, Tolstoy always considered that Sonya's outstanding qualities were her unusual simplicity of manner, directness, and sincerity.

2

In the spring of 1861 the two elder girls, Elizabeth and Sonya, passed their examinations for the University of Moscow. This was not expected of the younger sister, Tatyana. Her parents had great hopes for her remarkable voice and dreamed of giving her the opportunity of studying at the conservatory of music. The university examination marked the transition from childhood to youth. The girls began to wear long dresses and to appear in society. Each had a favorite dance—a characteristic detail. Elizabeth liked the lancers, Sonya the waltz, and Tatyana the mazurka.

In the meantime their family life went on as usual. There were always guests in the hospitable Behrs household. Usually on Saturdays and Sundays at least twenty people sat down at the dinner table. On such occasions the "Anke pie" was invariably served—the same pie that later made its appearance in Yasnaya Polyana and which, in Tolstoy's mind, became a symbol of the filled cup and of the material well-being of the privileged classes. The recipe for making this pie had been given to Mrs. Behrs by Dr. Anke, the dean of the medical school at the University of Moscow and a distant relative and good friend of Dr. Behrs. The pie became a tradition, and was served whenever the family was celebrating.

A number of young people were always among the visitors. Alexander, Dr. Behrs's eldest son, was a cadet in a military academy, and when he came home on leave he always brought several friends with him. The Behrses had many young relatives who frequently visited them for weeks on end during the Christmas and Easter vacations In the summer the same noisy crowd of young people gathered in Pokrovskoye, a country resort on the outskirts of Moscow. An unusual holiday spirit of gaiety and romantic love prevailed at these half-nursery, half-drawing-room gatherings. Tolstoy gave a remarkable picture of them in the chapters of *War and Peace* in which he introduces his readers to the life led by the Rostovs.

Sonya's first admirer was the student-teacher who had attempted to "convert" her. The lively, quick "nihilist" wore glasses and combed his long, shaggy hair straight back. But the practical young lady remained indifferent to the sighs of the poor "teacher." Once, in helping her to move something, he seized her hand and kissed it.

"How dare you?" was all she said, and to make her contempt evident she took her handkerchief and wiped the place that had been touched by his lips.

Determined complaints to her mother followed. But the girl's manner must have been somewhat flirtatious and provoking, for her mother's only comment was, "Why don't you follow Elizabeth's example? Nothing like that would ever happen to her!"

Next, the "nihilist's" place was taken by Mitrofan Polivanov, a senior classman at a military academy. He belonged to a wealthy and noble family and had excellent connections. This time Sonya's heart was not indifferent. When, at a rehearsal for amateur theatricals, the young man kissed her hands, she made no attempt to pull them away. This innocent romance lasted for a long time. When Polivanov was leaving for Petersburg to do some postgraduate work, he proposed and was accepted, but he asked Sonya to consider herself free and not to feel under any obligation. All this was more or less childish. Their elders could only guess at the young people's secrets. Tatyana, the youngest girl, had a secret of her own. Games with her doll Mimi had been replaced by romantic dreams about her cousin Kuzminsky, a very correct and proper law student whom she was planning to marry.

This was the situation when the exceptionally complex character of Lev Tolstoy was introduced into this world of middle-class Moscow young ladies, absorbed in flirtations and ribbons, and filled with all the poetry and stupidity of youth. The introduction had a momentous influence on the great writer's life.

Chapter Three

ONE DAY in May, 1856, a carriage stopped in front of the Behrs house in Pokrovskoye. Three "guests of honor" climbed the steps to the verandah: "Uncle Kostya" Islavin, Mrs. Behrs's brother; Baron Mengden; and an army officer, Count Lev Tolstoy. Their unexpected arrival created a commotion. The dinner had long been finished, all the servants were at church, and the guests were hungry. Dr. Behrs's handsome daughters received their majestic and imperturbable mother's permission to set the table and to serve the guests with what they could find. Delighted with this unusual assignment, the two eldest girls, the thirteen-year-old Elizabeth and the twelve-year-old Sonya, hovered gaily around the table. The little ten-year-old Tatyana was on the verge of tears—her sisters positively refused to let her take part in this interesting game.

After dinner the host eagerly asked Count Tolstoy about the war and about Sevastopol. Someone mentioned one of the "Sevastopol Songs," which were ascribed to Tolstoy and which had caused him trouble in Petersburg.

Everybody wanted to hear it. Islavin sat down at the piano and began to play the accompaniment. Tolstoy refused to sing. At that moment little Tatyana, who already displayed a remarkable musical talent, appeared on the scene. She was taught the words of the first verse, and, laughingly, Tolstoy sang a duet with the ten-year-old girl. This was followed by conversation about *Childhood* and *Boyhood*. All the characters in them were discussed. Everything about them was dear to both families. The girls listened attentively to the talk about the stories, which they already knew and liked.

Later everybody went for a walk. The "guests of honor" amused themselves and played leapfrog. . . .

That evening, in Moscow, Tolstoy wrote in his diary, "Had dinner at the Behrses with Kostya. The children served at the table. What delightful, gay girls!"

2

In the summer of 1861 Tolstoy returned to Russia after his second trip abroad. Although a lot of work awaited him in the country, he escaped to Moscow. He called on the Behrses and was tremendously surprised at the change there. The two eldest girls had passed their examinations, wore long dresses, put up their hair, and appeared in society. Tolstoy became a frequent and interested visitor. He stopped by in the afternoons, in the evenings, and for dinner, and almost at once became a part of the family. He talked about literature with the serious Elizabeth and suggested articles on Luther and Mohammed, which she wrote for his school and which later appeared in the supplements to his magazine. With the sentimental Sonya Tolstoy played four-hand arrangements on the piano, sat over a game of chess and spoke with animation about his pet pupils. With "the little devil" Tatyana he played all sorts of pranks, rode her on his back around the rooms, gave her puzzles to solve, and made her recite poetry. Sometimes he gathered everybody—the family and the guests—around the piano, and taught them to sing songs and chant prayers. He was particularly fond of young Tatyana's voice (she was then fourteen), often played accompaniments for her, brought her new music, and called her "Madame Viardot" [1] or "holiday girl" because she was always so gay.

Sometimes Tolstoy improvised a plot for an opera and made the young people write the words ("the less sense, the better"), which they sang to well-known tunes.

On one occasion he brought a story of Turgenev's, *First Love*, read it aloud beautifully to the girls, then said, "The love of the sixteen-year-old son—of the youth—is real love, which a man

---

[1] A celebrated singer of the period.

experiences only once in a lifetime, but the love of the father is rotten and immoral."

He arranged picnics and excursions and for hours at a time pointed out places of interest in Moscow, until the young people were completely exhausted. Sometimes he sneaked away to the nursery or to the kitchen, where he talked to the servants, and soon he was everyone's favorite.

Tolstoy's frequent visits became a topic of conversation around town. Rumor had it that he would marry the eldest sister, Elizabeth. Someone said that he had told his sister, "If I ever marry, I will marry one of the Behrses."

"Well, marry Elizabeth," the Countess was said to have answered. "She is serious, dependable, has good manners, and will make a splendid wife."

The gossip reached the ears of the Behrs family. The parents could not hope for anything better. Without any dowry, their daughter would become a Countess and the wife of a wealthy landowner and a great writer. The mother, who was on friendly terms with Tolstoy's sister, was particularly eager for the match.

All the talk and gossip seemed to rouse the cool and calm Elizabeth from her sleep. She began to daydream, she paid much more attention to her appearance, and gradually convinced herself that *"le comte,"* as the Behrses called Tolstoy, was madly in love with her.

Tolstoy, sensing the atmosphere that was being created around him and which made it necessary for him to take some definite step, soon became tired of it, and on May 6, 1861, he wrote in his diary: "Spent a very pleasant day with the Behrses. I should never dare to marry Elizabeth." And later, on September 22: "Elizabeth Behrs tempts me; but I will not let it happen. Mere planning without any feeling is not enough."

The two younger sisters, full of life and gaiety, attracted him much more. Tatyana was still a child, but Sonya seemed to draw him more and more. She was becoming prettier every day. Polivanov—to whom she considered herself "engaged"—had received his commission and was doing postgraduate work in

Petersburg. She missed him, cried, and anxiously read his letters to her younger sister. But for some time her feminine instinct had been telling her that *le comte* was becoming more and more interested in her. With such brilliant possibilities opening before her, the memory of the young officer became dimmer and was almost extinguished. True, he had known her for a long time and knew her for what she really was, while Count Tolstoy still had to be won. . . . And it was so difficult always to be at your best and not to shock his tastes! . . . Besides she was suffering because everything was so indefinite and uncertain. Perhaps she was mistaken, and the people who believed that Tolstoy was in love with her sister were right? . . .

She suffered, but her feminine pride and her ambitious dreams persisted. Attracting the Count at times by her sentimental thoughtfulness, at others by her energy, her directness, and her liveliness, she at last surrendered to her feeling, and was willing to acknowledge to herself that she was in love with Tolstoy and not with Polivanov.

In February, 1862, Tolstoy too felt that he was "almost in love." One episode shows how much he was a part of the Behrs family at the time. He had long kept his passion for gambling under control, but occasionally it flared up with the old force. One evening at his club he met an officer who was stopping there, and lost a thousand rubles playing billiards. The debt had to be paid within twenty-four hours. He had no money. He at once went to Katkov, the editor of the *Russky Vestnik,* and for a thousand rubles sold him *The Cossacks,* which he had neither finished nor revised. He told the Behrses about it, and they all agreed that he had sold it too cheaply. Tolstoy had to confess his gambling debt. The girls ran to their rooms and cried bitterly about *le comte's* conduct.

A few months later Tolstoy again appeared at the Behrses'. He was sad, looked ill, and had a bad cough. He was on his way to the Tartar steppes for a rest cure. Passing through Moscow, he stopped to see the Behrses and to show them the two peasant boys he was taking with him.

When he left that evening, Sonya was extremely sad. She took longer than usual over her prayers. Quietly the younger sister asked her: "*Sonya, tu aimes le comte?*"

"*Je ne sais pas,*" the girl whispered, evidently not in the least surprised by the question. And later she added, "Oh, Tatyana! Two of his brothers died of tuberculosis! . . ."

That night she could not fall asleep for a long time. She whispered to herself and sobbed quietly so that she would not awaken her sister.

3

That summer was exceptionally gay in the house in Pokrovskoye. Relatives and friends from Moscow came to visit, as well as neighbors who had summer homes near by. Walks, games, charades, and amateur theatricals followed one another. The festivities seemed to have no end.

Amid all the entertaining Sonya found time to work on a story, which in the evenings she secretly read to her younger sister. The story was called "Natasha." Later Tatyana described the plot:

"The two leading men in the story were Prince Dublitsky and Smirnov. Dublitsky was a middle-aged, not very attractive, energetic, clever man with very few convictions. Smirnov was a very young man—about twenty-three—with very high ideals, and a calm, even disposition; he was very earnest and interested in his work. The heroine of the story was Helen, a beautiful young girl with large, dark eyes. She had an older sister, Zinaida, an unpleasant and cold blonde, and a younger sister, Natasha, fifteen years old, a slim and gay girl. Dublitsky visited their home without any thought of love. Smirnov was in love with Helen, and she was attracted to him. He proposed, but she could not decide. The parents objected to the marriage because of his youth. Smirnov had to leave on business and he suffered greatly. There were many incidents of secondary importance—such as the description of Zinaida's affection for Dublitsky, Natasha's pranks, her love for her cousin, and so on. Dublitsky continued to visit Helen's family. She was bewildered, she could not understand her feelings, and she refused to admit even to herself that she was beginning to fall in love with him. The thought of deceiving her sister and Smirnov tortured her. She tried to fight her emotions but they were too strong for her. Dublitsky seemed to be interested in her more than in her sister, and this made him even more attractive to her. But his unstable opinions tired her. His uncanny insight embarrassed her. Frequently in her own mind she compared him with Smirnov and said, 'Smirnov loves me in a simple, wholehearted way, and never demands anything from me.' Smirnov returned. Watching him suffer and feeling that she was falling in love with Dublitsky made her want to take the vows and enter a convent. Finally Helen arranged a match between Zinaida and Dublitsky and later married Smirnov."

The story is far from being naïve, and if Sonya wrote it with the intention of showing it to Tolstoy, for an eighteen-year-old girl she displayed a surprisingly practical and enterprising mind. The story is a halfway confession; it is a challenge to frankness; it gives an unfavorable characterization of a rival sister; and it has elements that can arouse jealousy and spur a man to action.

Early in August Tolstoy again appeared in Moscow. The rest cure had been successful and he was again in good health, though he seemed more excitable than usual. His pride had suffered a severe blow. One night in the early part of July, police officers had appeared in Yasnaya Polyana and frightened his sister and his old aunt. These "robbers, with faces and hands washed with perfumed soap," as Tolstoy called them, had made a thorough search of the house and gone carefully through all of Tolstoy's private letters and diaries. The reason is not very clear to this day. Among the students who helped Tolstoy with his school were several men who had been expelled from the universities for participating in disturbances of a political nature. Because of numerous complaints the activities of Tolstoy, who at that time still held an official position, were carefully watched. The presence of several secret-service agents in the neighborhood of Yasnaya Polyana indicates that the government was suspicious. In 1861, while Tolstoy was in London, he became very friendly with the "terrible" Herzen, and for almost a month they appeared everywhere together—a circumstance which could not have been unnoticed by the Russian government agents abroad. When proclamations and reprints of articles from Herzen's magazine, the *Kolokol*, began to appear in Russia, the police made an energetic search for secret printing establishments. The secluded location of Yasnaya Polyana and the suspicious gatherings of student-teachers there attracted the attention of the police.

Tolstoy was almost insane with rage. To his cousin at the imperial court he wrote, "I often say to myself it was lucky that I was not there. If I had been, I am sure I should be on trial for murder." The police promised to return. With a loaded gun, Tolstoy waited for them. He succeeded in reaching the Tsar with a letter in which he complained of this treatment, and Alexander II sent one of his aides with expressions of regret couched in modest terms.

As disagreeable as these events were, they could not compare with his inner disturbances. His position in the Behrs family was becoming more complicated daily. Elizabeth considered him her own in a calm and self-assured way. Tolstoy hated her, and had to exercise all his self-control in her presence.

Moreover, a newcomer had made an appearance in Pokrovskoye, to which Tolstoy frequently walked from Moscow—a distance of approximately twelve miles. The Behrses had met Professor Nile Popov, a dignified, slow-moving man of about thirty-five, with gray, expressive eyes. He spent much of his time in Sonya's company and often, while with the others, kept his eyes on the young girl's graceful figure and animated face. He rented a house about two miles from Pokrovskoye and never missed an opportunity of spending as much time as he could with the Behrses.

Mrs. Behrs said, "Popov likes Sonya very much."

Sonya was aware of this and in a gay and carefree manner

met the professor halfway. This attitude made her attraction for him stronger than ever. Their friendship had its effect on Tolstoy. Jealousy was awakened in him. Perhaps, as he had done in the past, he would have killed his feeling with doubts, introspection, and logic; but whipped up by jealousy, his emotions matured rapidly and he had no time to think. He tried to pretend that he was indifferent, but he loved her and was jealous of her with his entire being, while Sonya gaily jabbered with her professor on the steps of the house in Pokrovskoye.

Could this have been instinctive or conscious strategy on the young girl's part?

She told Tolstoy that, while he was away, she had written a story.

"A story? What made you write it? What is it about?"

"About our life."

"Has anyone read it?"

"I have read it to Tatyana."

"Will you let me read it?"

"No, I cannot."

Tolstoy insisted.

4

On August 6, Tolstoy left Moscow for Yasnaya Polyana. Mrs. Behrs had made plans to visit her father, Alexander Islenyev, a portrait of whom Tolstoy has drawn in his *Childhood, Boyhood,* and *Youth.* After having lost all his property gambling, Islenyev was living in Ivitsi, the country estate of his second wife. Ivitsi was only forty miles from Yasnaya Polyana, and Tolstoy made Mrs. Behrs promise that on her way there she would stop overnight to visit his sister, Countess Mary.

The Behrs family arrived in Yasnaya Polyana in the evening. Tolstoy was touching and ridiculous as he worried about the arrangements for supper and awkwardly helped the maid make beds for the girls. The next day they had a picnic at Zaseka, an old government forest reservation, which bordered on Yasnaya

Polyana. Rugs were spread in a large clearing in the forest. Countess Tolstoy and Mrs. Behrs were busy with the samovar and the food they had brought. Tolstoy and the younger people climbed a huge haystack. When they were seated on top, he organized a chorus—a number of guests from the neighboring estates was present—and directed it with great animation.

The life in Ivitsi was a continuous round of festivities: dances, games, and visiting back and forth. On the third evening Tolstoy surprised everyone by appearing astride a white horse. He had become lonesome without the fresh voices and the laughter of his guests and had ridden forty miles from Yasnaya Polyana to see them. He was fresh, lively, and appeared to have reached a decision. He was more than usually attentive to Sonya. The young girl responded to his moods and blushed noticeably in his presence. Her eyes seemed to say, "I want to love you, but I am afraid. . . ."

Even the phlegmatic Elizabeth became nervous. Sobbing, she said to her youngest sister, "Tatyana, Sonya is trying to get *le comte* away from me. Can't you see it? Her manner, her eyes, her desire to be alone with him are obvious. . . ."

Finally Tolstoy and Sonya reached a point where they had to speak.

In her reminiscences, Tatyana has described the scene:

"In the evening, after supper, I was asked to sing. This was the last thing I wanted to do, so I tried to find a hiding place and ran into the drawing room. I hid under the piano. The room was empty, except for a card table that had been left after a game.

"A few minutes later Sonya and Tolstoy entered. They seemed unusually excited as they sat down at the card table.

" 'So you are leaving tomorrow?' Sonya asked. 'Why so soon? We shall miss you!'

" 'Mary is alone and she is getting ready to go abroad.'

" 'Shall you go with her?'

" 'No, I wanted to, but now I cannot go.'

"Sonya refrained from asking him why. She could guess the

answer. I saw by the expression on her face that something important was about to happen. I wanted to come out of my hiding place but I was ashamed and remained silent.

" 'Let's go into the hall,' Sonya said. 'They will be looking for us.'

" 'No, wait a moment, please! It's so nice in here.'

"With a piece of chalk, he was writing something on the table. In a voice vibrating with excitement, he asked, 'Can you read what I write to you, if I use only the first letter of every word?'

"Looking him straight in the eye, Sonya answered, 'I believe I can. . . .'

"Then followed the famous correspondence, which is known to everyone who has read *Anna Karenina*.

"Tolstoy wrote, 'Y.y.a.y.d.f.h.r.m.t.f.o.m. o.a.a.o.t.i.o.h.'

"As if inspired, my sister read, 'Your youth and your desire for happiness remind me too forcibly of my old age and of the impossibility of happiness.'

"Tolstoy had to prompt her in several places.

" 'Try it again,' he said. 'T.i.a.m.i.y.f.a.y.s.E.a.m. Y.a.T.w.h.t. h.m.'

" 'There is a misconception in your family about your sister Elizabeth and me. You and Tatyana will have to help me.' . . ."

On their return journey the Behrses again spent two or three days in Yasnaya Polyana and then, in company with Countess Mary Tolstoy, who was going abroad, set out for Moscow.

At Tula, Tolstoy unexpectedly appeared, dressed in traveling clothes. Everyone was delighted to learn that he, too, was going to Moscow.

In Moscow difficult days began for Tolstoy. He tried to write articles for his educational magazine, he went to the theater, and he made calls, but he felt himself more and more drawn to the Behrses. At first he controlled his desire and called only every two or three days, but finally he gave up the struggle and appeared every day. He had a feeling that his frequent visits were a nuisance; he felt uncomfortable, but he could not stay away. At times Sonya gave him a gay and cheerful welcome, at others she was sad and dreamy, and then again she seemed stern and angry. The constant strain exhausted him and he suffered from uncertainty. At last she let him read her story. This stimulant failed to have the immediate effect she expected. Tolstoy could not reach a decision. He doubted, and he tried to test himself. His inherent pride made him dread the possibility of a refusal. When great men are ill, or when they are in love, they behave like other mortals. Though there was nothing unusual about her, the lively, clever, eighteen-year-old girl held the genius in the hollow of her hand. Fate and circumstances had decreed that she was to be the ruling power in his complex spiritual life. He believed that he could not have any happiness without her, and for the time being, the desire to win her love was the only aim of his life.

One of Tolstoy's biographers was baffled by this situation. Why had the great writer failed to display his usual insight on this occasion? Why had he demanded so much from Valeria Arsenyev, and why was love the only thing he expected from Sonya Behrs?

Why? . . . He had tried to change Valeria Arsenyev and to make her a suitable wife.

He loved Sonya Behrs and he longed for her with his whole passionate being.

5

Here are some excerpts from Tolstoy's diaries of the period. They reflect his emotions better than anything else.

"August 23. Spent the evening with the Behrses. A mere child! A beautiful thing! How complicated everything is! If I could only find a clear and honest path. . . . I am afraid of myself. What if this is only the search for love, and not real love! I try to see only her bad traits. A mere child! A lovely thing! . . .

"August 26. Walked over to the Behrses. Quiet, comfortable. Girlish laughter. Sonya was not very amiable—bad-mannered, but amusing. Let me read her story. What dynamic truth and simplicity! Uncertainty torments her. I read everything calmly, without any jealousy or envy, but the 'not very attractive,' and the 'very few convictions' hurt me. I am calm now. She was not writing about me. . . .

"August 28.[2] I am thirty-four. A repulsive face. Should not think of marriage! I have another calling in life, and that is why so much has been given me. . . .

"August 30. I am not jealous of Popov. I am the one. A stroll, a summer house, supper at home, eyes, and the night! . . . Fool! Not intended for me, but I am in love as much as I was with Sonya Koloshin and with Alexandra Obolensky. That is all. . . .

"September 2. Called at the Behrses. . . . The situation with Elizabeth is terrible. So nice with Sonya. . . . She mentioned Popov and her blouse. . . . Can it all be a coincidence? . . .

"September 3. There again; nothing at first, then a stroll. Lorgnette: 'He is not very attractive, and you are wholesome, please come to see us!' I am calm! Rode home thinking: it's natural, or it's exceptionally sensitive feeling, or it's the most conventional flirting—one today, and another tomorrow—or it's natural and sensitive and flirtatious. Nothing, nothing at all! Silence! Never before have I imagined my future with a wife so calmly, so gaily, or so clearly. . . .

"September 6. I am too old to play games. Leave, or be cut asunder. . . .

"September 7. . . . Dublitsky! I should not stick my nose in youth, poetry, beauty, or love. . . . For cadets only, my boy! . . .

"On the tenth of September awoke at ten—exhausted by the excitement of the preceding night. Worked lazily, and, like a schoolboy waiting for Sunday, waited for the evening. . . . To the Kremlin. . . . She was not at home. . . . She came in looking haughty and serious. I left, feeling hopeless and more than ever in love. *Au fond*, there is no hope. I must . . . I must cut this knot in two. I feel sorry for Elizabeth and at the same time

[2] Tolstoy's birthday.

I hate her. O Lord! help me and guide me! I feel another sleepless night of torture is here—I who laughed at the tortures of people in love! . . . If you make fun of something, it is certain to catch up with you. How often I have planned to tell her, to tell Tatyana, and all to no avail. . . . I have begun to hate Elizabeth with all my soul. O Lord, help me, guide me! O Mother of God, help me! . . .

"September 12. I am in love as I never believed anyone could be in love. I am mad. I will shoot myself if things go on this way. They danced. She is absolutely wonderful. I am the repulsive Dublitsky. I should have known it before. Too late to stop now. Dublitsky! Who cares! My love makes me beautiful. Yes. Tomorrow morning I will go there. I had fleeting moments, but I failed to take advantage of them. I was afraid. . . .

"September 13. Nothing happened. . . . Each day I think that I cannot suffer or be happy any longer and each day I become more insane. Again left there with sadness, remorse, and happiness in my soul. Tomorrow as soon as I am up, I will go there, and I will tell her everything. Or . . . it's four in the morning. I have written her a letter, and I will give it to her tomorrow. That is, today, the fourteenth. O God, how afraid I am that I will die! Such happiness seems impossible to me. O Lord, help me!

"September 15. I failed to tell her, but I told her that there was something I had to tell her. Tomorrow . . ."

"Tomorrow" came at last.

Tolstoy arrived in the evening. He was visibly excited. He sat down at the piano, but rose without finishing what he was playing, and started to pace the floor. At last he walked over to Sonya and asked her to play an arrangement for four hands with him. She agreed, but instead of playing he said, "Let's just sit here."

They were sitting close to one another on the piano bench and Sonya was gently playing the accompaniment to the "Il Bacio" waltz.

Evidently Tolstoy's excitement was embarrassingly contagious. She addressed her sister, who was walking through the room, "Tatyana, try to sing the waltz; I believe I can play the accompaniment now."

Tatyana stopped in the middle of the room and waited.

Suddenly Tolstoy's face darkened. Once more the opportunity to speak was slipping away, but in his pocket was the letter he had written to her, and he decided to give it to her if he could not find another opportunity to speak. Sonya was nervous and could not play the accompaniment. Tolstoy replaced her at the piano.

He came to a decision. "If Tatyana takes the last high note clearly, I will give Sonya the letter tonight. If not, I will keep the letter."

Tatyana was in good form, and at the end took the last high note in a clear, strong voice. Excitedly, Tolstoy said, "You sing beautifully tonight!"

Tatyana was called away to help with the tea.

Still unable to speak, Tolstoy gave Sonya the letter. He told her that he would wait for an answer in her mother's room.

Frightened, Sonya ran to her room and locked the door behind her.

The letter read:

"Sonya:

"I cannot bear this any longer! Every day for the last three weeks I have told myself I will tell her everything today, and every day I leave with the same sadness, remorse, fear, and happiness in my soul. Every night I think about what has happened, and I suffer and ask myself: why haven't I told her and how and what would I have said? I am taking this letter along, and I will give it to you if I again do not have the courage or the opportunity to tell you everything. I believe that your family is laboring under a false impression. They all seem to think that I am in love with your sister Elizabeth. That is not true. Your story is constantly in my mind, because after having read it, I became convinced that it is unfair for me, Dublitsky, to dream of happiness. . . . That your conception of love is too romantic. . . . That I never have been and never would be jealous of the person you love. I believe that I would enjoy you as I enjoy children. When we were in Ivitsi, I wrote, 'Your presence reminds me too vividly of my age, and of the impossibility of happiness—your presence. . . .'

"But then and ever since I have been lying to myself. Then I still could have stopped, and retired once again into the cloister of my solitary labors and interest in my work. Now I cannot, and I feel that I have made trouble in your family, and that my forthright, precious relations with you as a friend and honest human being have been lost. I cannot leave, and I dare not stay. You are an honest person. Put your hand upon your heart and deliberately—for God's sake deliberately!—tell me what I am to do. Making fun of something is certain to bring it home to you. A month ago, if anyone had told me that I could suffer as I have suffered, and be happy suffering, I should have died laughing. Tell me honestly if you want to be my wife? But only if you can say it with conviction and from the bottom of your heart. If you have even a shadow of a doubt, say no. For God's sake, examine your heart carefully. A 'no' from you will be terrible, but I am prepared for it and I will find strength to accept it. . . . But when I am your husband, it will be horrible if I shall never be loved as I love you. . . ."

A determined knocking at the door interrupted the reading of the letter. Elizabeth was almost beside herself.

"Sonya! Open the door! Open it immediately! I must talk to you!"

The door opened.

"What has *le comte* written to you? Tell me!"

Sonya stood silent, with the letter in her hand. In an excited, imperious voice Elizabeth screamed, "Tell me at once what *le comte* has written to you!"

Quietly, Sonya answered, "*Il m'a fait la proposition.*"

Sobbing, the eldest sister whispered, "Refuse him! Refuse him instantly!"

Sonya was silent.

The mother appeared and with some difficulty put an end to the disagreeable scene.

In the meantime, in Mrs. Behrs's small drawing room, Tolstoy was waiting impatiently. With his hands clasped behind his back, he stood leaning against the stove. His face was serious, the expression in his eyes preoccupied, and he looked paler than usual.

At last he heard light footsteps. . . . Quickly Sonya walked into the room and said, "Yes!"

A few minutes later they were being congratulated.

The old doctor was ill and had locked himself in his room. When he learned about the proposal from his wife, he was at first antagonistic. He was under the impression that Tolstoy was in love with Elizabeth and that the love was mutual. He felt strongly for his eldest daughter, and for the first few minutes refused to give his consent. But Sonya's tears and Elizabeth's noble-spirited plea soon put an end to his opposition. The parents gave their consent, and in his diary for September 17, Tolstoy wrote, "Bridegroom, presents, champagne; Elizabeth is pitiful and depressing. She should hate me. Instead she kisses me. . . ."

Tolstoy had insisted on having the wedding in a week, and the Behrses had agreed. A rush began which is fully described in *Anna Karenina*.

On September 24, Tolstoy wrote in his diary, "I cannot understand where this week has gone. I cannot remember anything; only a kiss at the piano, the flash of satin, and then the jealousy of the past, doubts of her love, and a thought that she is fooling herself. . . ."

He also wrote of the "fear, the doubts, and the urge to run away" which took possession of him on his wedding day.

Other sources supply other details.

Like Levin in *Anna Karenina*, Tolstoy gave his bride the diaries he had kept over the years. She read about all his past infatuations and affairs and cried bitterly over the "horrid" notebooks.

Many other details appeared later in Levin's wedding.

Tatyana wrote, "The 23rd of September came at last. Entirely unexpectedly Tolstoy arrived in the morning. He came straight to our room. Elizabeth was not at home, and after exchanging greetings, I went upstairs. A little later when I saw mother, I told her that Tolstoy was in our room. She was very much surprised, and annoyed. The groom was not expected to see the bride on the wedding day. Mother went downstairs and found them among the trunks, suitcases, and things waiting to be packed. Sonya was in tears. Mother made no attempt to find out why Sonya was crying. She spoke very sternly to Tolstoy, insisted that he leave at once, and made him go. Sonya told me that he had been assailed by doubts and had not slept all night. He wanted to learn from her if she loved him. Perhaps her memories of Polivanov, who had just then most inopportunely appeared in Moscow, and of the past tormented her? Would it be better and more honest to stop before it was too late? No matter how hard Sonya tried, she could not convince him."

All these details fit in with familiar pictures in *Anna Karenina*. Even the episode of the dress shirt, which delayed the wedding for an hour and a half, was taken from real life. The famous English critic, Matthew Arnold, has expressed surprise that Tolstoy should have used such a scene, which, though possible, seemed so improbable. In drawing on his own experiences when he was describing Levin's wedding, Tolstoy was evidently reluctant to neglect this detail, which had caused so much worry and excitement.

But it is a mistake to look for an exact counterpart of Tolstoy's romance in Kitty's relations with Levin. True, a Russian critic, Gromyko, based his analysis of *Anna Karenina* on the assumption that Tolstoy and Levin were the same person. Tolstoy neither affirmed nor denied the assumption, but expressed the opinion that Gromyko's was the best interpretation of his novel. However, Levin lacks Tolstoy's genius, and is therefore at times quite boring.

As usual, in portraying Sonya as Kitty, Tolstoy embellished her by supplying her with a patriarchal, aristocratic family.

Kitty's portrait is much closer to Tolstoy's ideal wife at that time than to reality. The relations of the two couples also differ in other respects. The rich, aristocratic Princess Shcherbatsky, in marrying Constantine Levin, followed only the dictates of her heart. The relations between the daughter of Dr. Behrs and the famous, financially independent writer, Count Lev Tolstoy, were much more involved and complex.

The wedding was solemnized on the evening of September 23 in the Kremlin, in the palace church, which was filled with guests. Tolstoy noticed that the bride looked as if she had been crying. Polivanov was one of the ushers. Tolstoy's brother, Count Sergei, had left for Yasnaya Polyana to prepare everything for the arrival of the bride and groom.

After the usual formal reception and champagne at the Behrs home, Sonya changed into a dark-blue traveling dress. Tolstoy's closed coach with six horses, a coachman, and an outrider was waiting at the door.

In accordance with the old Russian custom, everyone sat for a few seconds in silence before the departure.

A touching parting. The couple climbed into the coach. Barbara, the Behrses' old maid, and Alexis, Tolstoy's manservant, sat in the back seat, outside. Everyone came out on the porch for the farewells. Last kisses, last wishes—and swaying from side to side, the heavy coach was under way, carrying with it Tolstoy and his fate. The day was dark and raw. A disagreeable, autumn rain was in the air.

Chapter Four

IN YASNAYA POLYANA, the couple were met by "Auntie" Tatyana Yergolsky and Count Sergei Tolstoy.

The charming old lady was a distant relative of the Tolstoys, and played an important part in their life. The warmest and most tender passages of Tolstoy's *Reminiscences* are devoted to her and to her fate. She grew up in the family of Tolstoy's grandfather, who provided for her education. As a young girl, with thick braids of dark, curly hair, large lively eyes, an energetic disposition, and an unusually kind, courageous heart, she had been very charming. Small wonder that Tolstoy's father, who grew up with her, formed a tender attachment for her and proposed to her. The feeling was mutual. In the pages of *War and Peace* this romance of the author's father is reflected in the relations between Count Nicholas Rostov and Sonya. In real life, as in the novel, the poor girl had to resign in favor of a more fortunate rival, helping her with her household duties. Eight years later, Countess Mary Tolstoy died, leaving her husband with five children. Miss Yergolsky devoted the rest of her life to their care. Another six years went by and Count Nicholas Tolstoy proposed to her again. Unwilling to spoil her relations with the children or with him, she refused, and remained an old maid.

Tatyana Yergolsky was very religious, loved music, and played the piano well. She lavished all her love for Count Nicholas Tolstoy on his children. She was particularly fond of Lev, and in her last years she linked him completely with the one whom she had loved all her life.

In the nineties, Tolstoy wrote, "The purpose of her existence was love, and she had no reason to hurry. These two qualities, love and ease, imperceptibly drew people closer to her, and lent a special charm to her presence."

The dream of her life was to see her "dear" Lev happy in marriage. They corresponded about it while Tolstoy was still serving in the Caucasus, and he was often so deeply touched by her tender letters that he cried.

The serene joy with which the charming old lady of sixty-seven greeted the couple can easily be understood.

Even the proud, reserved, self-sufficient eldest brother, Count Sergei, appeared to be moved on the occasion.

Events had moved so fast that Count Sergei, who had gone to the country to prepare for the arrival of Tolstoy and his bride, had had time to redecorate only the room for his new sister-in-law.

The house in which Tolstoy had been born was no longer part of the estate. The huge, palatial home, with thirty-six rooms, white columns, and beautifully kept gardens, had been sold in the days when Tolstoy had gambled for high stakes and had needed money.

Out of the old splendor only two small buildings remained. These had been wings of the great house that had been removed. In one of them was the school for the peasant children. In the other Tolstoy and his bride made their home. Their abode had no trace of luxury. All the furniture was hard and plain. The table service was unpretentious. The kitchen and the servants' rooms were lighted with tallow, and the other rooms with palm-oil candles. Oil lamps were used only on special occasions. Tolstoy changed from his fashionable clothes, made by Charmeur, to a warm shirt, such as later became a part of his traditional costume.

Though she was not accustomed to luxury, his wife was surprised by some of the things she saw. For instance, he always slept with his head on a pillow of red Russian leather, which looked like a seat that had been taken out of a carriage, and he never used a pillowcase. None of the bedrooms had rugs because everyone had warm slippers. No flowers were grown in the garden, the paths were never swept, and the house was surrounded with tall weeds, into which the servants unceremoniously threw all the refuse.

The staff of servants was small: Dunya, the maid; Alexis, the manservant; and a cook, an old man who never remained sober for long.

According to Fet, into this stern atmosphere "came flying a beautiful bird who enlivened everything by her presence."

Proudly wearing a lace bonnet with dark-red ribbons, the young Countess tried to play the part of a serious and dignified hostess and of a great lady. "Not at all badly! She seems natural, and that's splendid!" Tolstoy recorded.

Occasionally she became tired of her role. The stillness of the house made her nervous. An uncontrollable desire to move and to be gay took possession of her. She ran, jumped, and thought about the days when she had played with her younger sister, Tatyana, who loved to run and scream that "something" was chasing her.

From the beginning the Countess tried to help her husband. She stopped in the school to watch the classes and helped one child with a composition and another with a problem. Best of all she liked the picnics with the school children. They stopped somewhere, played games, sang songs, and enjoyed themselves.

She tried to help with the farm and went to watch the cows being milked. To Tolstoy's great amazement the smell of the barn made her sick, and the young city girl could not force herself to work with the livestock.

She wrote to her sister, "Auntie seems to be very happy, Sergei is very nice, and I see no reason even to mention Lev. Tatyana, he loves me so much that I feel ashamed and terrified because there is no reason for it! . . ."

Occasionally they wrote letters together:

Count: "Tatyana, dear friend, please sympathize with me: I have a stupid wife."

Countess: "He is stupid, too, Tatyana."

Count: "This startling revelation that we are both stupid will be quite a disappointment to you. But every disappointment is followed by something pleasant. We are both glad that we are stupid and we have no desire to be anything else."

Countess: "I want him to be clever."

Count: "That certainly is a surprise! You realize that we are rolling with laughter while we are writing this? . . ."

They amused each other like little children. They were happy.

On January 5, 1863, Tolstoy wrote in his diary, "I love her when she awakens at night or in the morning and when I see that she is looking at me and that she loves me. No one, and least of all I, could prevent her from loving in her own way, in the way she knows how. I love her when we sit closely, and know that we love one another in our own way. When she says, 'Lev! . . .' and stops—'Why were the chimneys of the fireplaces built so straight?' Or, 'Why do horses live so long?' I love her when we are alone. 'What shall we do? Sonya, what shall we do?' She laughs. I love her when she is angry at me and for a second has a harsh thought or even a harsh word for me, 'Leave me alone! I am bored!' A minute later she is already smiling shyly at me. I love her when she cannot see me and when she is not aware of it. I love her in my own way. I love her when, like a little girl in a yellow dress, she sticks out her tongue and her chin. I love her when her head is thrown back and I can see her serious, frightened, childish, and passionate face. I love her when . . ."

According to Tolstoy it was "incredible, breath-taking happiness."

He was beside himself and had to share his delight with Countess Alexandra Tolstoy:

"I am writing from the country and while I am writing I can hear the voice of my wife upstairs. She is talking to my brother. I love her more than anyone in this world. I had reached the age of thirty-four without realizing that one could love so much or be so happy. I will write you a long letter when I am calmer. 'Calmer' is not the right word because my mind is calmer and clearer than it has ever been in my life, but when I am more accustomed. Now I have a constant feeling that I have stolen an undeserved, unlawful happiness that was not intended for me. Here she comes now, I hear her steps, and I feel elated. Thank you for your last letter. Why should people as good as you—and what is even more surprising, a being like my wife— love me? . . ."

Yet, when the Tolstoys went to Moscow for a short visit in December, 1862, outsiders sensed a certain change in them. They no longer exchanged restless, inquisitive, loving glances. He displayed a tender thoughtfulness for her and she accepted it with resignation. Temporarily the Countess's energetic, independent nature was entirely overshadowed by Tolstoy's prestige. The young woman repeated the words and thought the thoughts of her great husband.

The Tolstoys spent only a few weeks in Moscow. They were anxious to return to their country solitude, where they could once more enjoy their extraordinary happiness without outside interferences.

Three and a half months after their wedding, on January 5, 1863, Tolstoy wrote in his diary, "My happiness seems to absorb me completely. . . . I often think that such happiness, with all its peculiar characteristics, will pass, and no one is or will be aware of it, though no one will experience anything like it, and only I am conscious of it."

But the beautiful idyl of the Tolstoys was noticed, and by everyone. In his reminiscences, written at an advanced age, Fet mentioned it with touching sympathy and tenderness, and one of Countess Tolstoy's brothers wrote: "While I was at Yasnaya Polyana, I was perhaps the closest observer of their family life. Their understanding, their friendship, and their mutual love always served for me as an example and as an ideal of marital happiness. All I need to say is that my parents, who, like all parents, were never satisfied with the fates of their children, frequently said, 'We could not wish anything better for Sonya!' "

2

But fate had not only roses in store for them. There were outbursts of temper, scenes, and misunderstandings. The young wife was not the only one who cried. The thirty-four-year-old Tolstoy cried too, thinking bitterly that they were "like all the others." He was afraid of these "unnecessary" scratches, which outraged his feeling for her and which seemed to leave ugly scars on the delicate fabric of their happiness. Like Levin in *Anna Karenina*, he was already learning to yield, to wait, and to conquer his desire of proving that he was right. . . . Why be rash? Ridiculous to be angry with oneself. . . . In his eyes they were meant to be one forever.

While she was pregnant, the outbursts of temper and the scenes became more frequent. Though he was unusually understanding, for a long time he could not realize the purely physiological causes of their frequent quarrels. Later, in the *Kreutzer Sonata*, he considered this problem in a merciless, cynical light. During the first years of married life he was ready to blame everything on his young wife.

Troubles melted away like light, fluffy clouds in a hot, blue sky. Their recurring attacks of jealousy proved to be a much more serious threat to their happiness. They were both jealous by nature. They were jealous without any reason, and with that incomprehensible sharpness of feeling which can be explained only in the light of their passionate temperaments. These attacks of jealousy blinded them, made them unjust to each other, and caused them deep suffering.

Quarrels of this kind began very soon. A letter had to be written to Countess Alexandra Tolstoy. For the time being introductions had to be made by mail. The young wife was jealous and had no desire to write. On October 1 Tolstoy wrote in his diary, "She would rather not write to my cousins at court, she suspects everything." Four days later he succeeded in persuading

‚her, but the cold, forced, polite French letter she wrote made him bitter and angry.

Calls had to be made in Moscow. She protested. She particularly disliked the idea of calling on Princess Alexandra Obolensky, with whom Tolstoy had been in love. Nevertheless they called, and the Countess, who had been warmly and cordially received everywhere, could not restrain her malice and wrote in her diary, "We also called on A. A. Obolensky, M. A. Sukhotin, and E. A. Zhemchuzhnikov. The first two had nothing except contempt for the young and stupid wife of their former admirer and frequent guest, Lev Tolstoy!"

When he went out without her in the evenings, she waited calmly until the hour he had set for his return, but the least delay upset her. Jealous suspicions were ever present. She had a particularly bitter feeling toward Tolstoy's old flame, Princess Alexandra Obolensky. On one occasion he was spending an evening with Aksakov, at whose house he met Zavalishin, who had participated in the December Uprising—at the time Tolstoy was gathering material for a novel of that period. They became engaged in an animated conversation, and he returned home at one-thirty, instead of midnight. The Countess was beside herself with jealousy and met him with a wild torrent of tears.

The country seemed a safe refuge from jealousy. But when her cousin, Olga Islenyev, visited them in Yasnaya Polyana and displayed her musical talents by playing duets with Tolstoy, the Countess felt envious and jealous, and began to hate her. After her husband's death she told V. F. Bulgakov how jealous she had been of the peasant women during the first years. She said that she had even dressed in peasant clothes and had walked for hours through the park and the surrounding forest, thinking that Tolstoy would mistake her for someone else, and would call her by the name she was so eager to learn.

Tolstoy was even more jealous. Polivanov's presence in Moscow, in January of 1863, was "distasteful" to him, though he tried to "bear it as well as possible." He wrote in his diary, "She says about jealousy: 'one must have respect,' 'one must trust,' and so forth. Nothing but words, and I am so afraid."

He was jealous of a teacher at the Yasnaya Polyana school and of a casual young visitor.

The Countess said to her sister, "The other day over a cup of tea, we had an animated argument with Erlenwein about something very unimportant, when suddenly Lev became jealous."

"Jealous of that teacher? Good Lord! I certainly had not expected that. All the teachers are so serious!"

"At first I had no idea that he was jealous. I could not understand his attitude and I asked myself: Why should he say such sarcastic things to me? Why should he treat me so coolly? I cried and could not find an answer."

This trivial episode assumed unwarranted proportions in Tolstoy's diary. Tolstoy suffered; he called on his entire married life as witness; he tried to be fair. Addressing his wife, he exclaimed, "Involuntarily I seek a way to hurt you. That is bad and it will not last. Don't be angry. I cannot help loving you. . . ." And further: "Today the obvious pleasure she derived from talking to Erlenwein and attracting his attention brought me back to the old height of truth and strength. I can read this over and say: Yes, I know, this is jealousy! This will calm me and do something else to throw me back into the conventional life that I have hated since my youth. I have been leading it for nine months. It is terrible! I am a gambler and a drunkard. I am on a spree of farming and I have wasted nine months, which could have been the best and which I have made almost the worst in my life. All I need to live happily is to be loved by her and by myself and instead, all this time, I have been hating myself. . . . I understand why she enjoys the company of another person no matter how insignificant and no matter how unbearable she makes me feel. I realize that during the last nine months I have been the most insignificant, the weakest, the most senseless, and the most conventional person."

How much ado about nothing! His fiery temperament seethed and boiled. His wife had exchanged a few lively words with a teacher, and he was ready to renounce himself and his happiness.

The amusing and tragic scene that Tolstoy described in *Anna Karenina* becomes more understandable in the light of his own reactions. Tatyana wrote:

"On one occasion Pissarev, a very pleasant, social-minded man whom we all knew, stopped at Yasnaya Polyana. He very seldom visited us. Sonya sat by the samovar pouring tea. Pissarev sat next to her. I believe this was his only sin. Pissarev helped Sonya pass the cups and made himself generally useful. He was gay, he joked and laughed a great deal, and every now and then he leaned toward her to exchange a few words.

"I was watching Tolstoy. Pale, and very much upset, he would rise, pace the floor, leave the room, only to reappear again. In some way his nervousness was contagious. Sonya became aware of it and was at a loss what to do.

"The situation came to a sudden end the next morning, when Tolstoy gave orders to get the coach ready, and the manservant informed the startled young man that the horses were waiting. . . .

"They were both painfully jealous and poisoned their lives by spoiling their good, friendly relations," wrote Tatyana.

3

The solitude in which the Tolstoys spent the first years of their married life is difficult to imagine. At that time the Moscow-Kursk-Kiev railroad had not been built, and traveling by coach was extremely complicated because of the terrible condition of the country roads. Once, or at the most twice, a year, Fet and his wife—on their way from Moscow to their country place— or Dyakov, the friend of Tolstoy's youth, stopped for a few days. Sometimes Count Sergei Tolstoy, Lev's only living brother, came to see them. Once in a great while the Auerbach family or the teacher and novelist Eugene Markov came down from Tula. But that was all. Tolstoy was inclined to look down on the neighboring landowners, and whenever any of them called, for old time's sake, on "Auntie" Yergolsky at Yasnaya Polyana, he invariably disappeared through the back door.

As a matter of fact, Tolstoy had no real friends. During his school years he became friendly with Dyakov, a classmate of his elder brother's. The trials and tribulations of this friendship are described in *Boyhood* and in *Youth*. Dyakov was a kind-hearted, witty, gay, practical person, with a carefree way of accepting the gifts life had sent him and who obviously had nothing in common with the Prince Neklyudov of the Tolstoy stories. That character was also taken from life, being, more or less, the portrait of Dmitri Tolstoy, Lev's brother who had died from tuberculosis in 1856. Tolstoy remained on good terms with Dyakov, but at the time of his wedding their friendship had already become a mere cordial association. At that stage Fet was Tolstoy's closest friend. Their friendship was perfectly natural. Fet was a retired cavalry officer. Turgenev thought him merely stupid. His miserliness became a byword. Wealth, which he craved, was in his opinion the only worth-while thing in life. He was extremely conservative, believed in serfdom, and was indignant with the government for the Act of Emancipation. Perhaps his extreme point of view was the reason for the harsh criticisms by Turgenev, who was a liberal. Actually Fet was undoubtedly far above most of his contemporaries, as well as a true poet who had contributed much to Russian literature. He was very sensitive to beauty in art. In his later years he translated into Russian a number of ancient classics, both parts of Goethe's *Faust*, and Schopenhauer's *The World as Will and Idea*. Though talented in his way, he had nothing in common with Tolstoy. But he adored and almost worshiped Tolstoy, and probably his unreserved admiration was the reason why Tolstoy was kindly disposed toward him.

Significantly, Tolstoy's later friendships with the philosopher Nicholas Strakhov, with the painter Gay, and with Chertkov had the same foundation.

Earlier in his life Tolstoy was convinced that friendship was possible only according to one formula: "Everything or nothing." But apparently even "everything" had to have a very definite character.

For entertainment, the Tolstoys had to depend on each other. The rapidly aging Miss Tatyana Yergolsky and the old maid who lived with her were not able to relieve their solitude. The only person who enlivened their monotonous existence was Tatyana, the Countess's younger sister. Beginning with the spring of 1863, she frequently came to Yasnaya Polyana, and stayed for weeks at a time. Everyone loved the "holiday girl." Tolstoy sensed her peculiar disposition and became attached to her as if she were his own sister. In 1862 he wrote to her, "I at once saw in it your beautiful, charming nature, full of laughter against a poetical and serious background. I should have to go a long way to find another Tatyana, but you too would be hard put to find another admirer like Lev Tolstoy." He eagerly watched this fiery, cheerful, self-sufficient girl, who, before his very eyes, was transformed into a beautiful young lady. Jokingly he told her, "You think you are not earning your board? I am constantly using you as material."

Tolstoy took his characters from real life, but they were never exact reproductions of the originals. For him "real life" served only as a starting point. For example, in *War and Peace* Natasha Rostov, with her passionate nature and romantic adventures, outwardly very much resembles Tatyana Behrs. But the sharp contours of that very earthly character were softened and romanticized by Tolstoy—who, in doing so, used the richest colors on his palette. The author put much of himself and of his genius into Natasha Rostov, and that is why she is one of the most charming heroines in Russian literature.

No wonder the Yasnaya Polyana recluses were startled by the sudden appearance of Baroness Mengden, who unexpectedly arrived from Tula to invite the Tolstoys to a ball. The heir to the Russian throne was expected in Tula, and the local nobility were making plans for an appropriate reception. For the sake of his sister-in-law, Tolstoy had to don full dress and serve as escort. Sadly the Countess excused herself because of ill health. In her reminiscences she wrote:

"Lev decided to take my sister, Tatyana, to the ball, and I settled down to the hard task of making her a dress. . . . When Lev, in full dress, left with Tatyana for Tula to attend the ball, I began to cry bitterly and cried all evening long. We led a monotonous, secluded, dull life, and when the opportunity arose, I—I was then only nineteen—I could not take advantage of it."

She said to her sister, "You know, Tatyana, even if I had been well, I could not have gone."

"Why?"

"Aren't you familiar enough with Lev's opinions? How could I have worn an evening dress? Unthinkable! How many times has he criticized married women, who, as he expresses it, 'expose' themselves."

This was a fleeting weakness, a sad mood. Generally speaking, the Countess endured her secluded country life courageously, even after the house had become filled with children.

At times life became too dull, too shut in. A peaceful haven reached at the age of eighteen has few attractions. People crave the open sea, people crave storms. On March 3, 1863, Tolstoy jotted down in his diary, "I fear this mood more than anything else in this world." And on January 23, 1863: "Often, and particularly now, I fear the many things in me she dislikes, and cannot understand. Because of me, she forces herself in numerous ways, and instinctively holds these sacrifices against me."

He realized that some variety was necessary in their mode of life. At the same time he was opposed to long sojourns in Moscow.

He wrote to his father-in-law, "I often dream of having an apartment in Moscow. To send our baggage over the winter roads, and to spend three or four months in Moscow in our own little world brought with us from Yasnaya Polyana: the same Alexis, the same nurse, the same samovar, the same everything. You, your world, the theater, music, books, a library—this has recently become most important of all to me—an occasional conversation with a new and interesting man—these are the things we lack in Yasnaya Polyana. The need to count every penny and to be afraid that we will not have enough money for this or that, the desire to buy and the inability to do so, and, worst of all, the feeling of shame because everything in our home is shabby and run-down—this, perhaps, is more important than anything else. Until I am able to put aside an adequate amount—at least six thousand rubles—the visit to Moscow will have to remain a dream."

In order to be able to "put aside" the necessary amount, he went in, with his usual enthusiasm, for intensive farming.

He bought bees, built a number of hives about two miles from the house, and, with a net over his face, sat for hours watching them and studying their life. He bred thoroughbred sheep, and insisted that he would not be happy until he had acquired some Japanese hogs. When they finally arrived, he was delighted and wrote, "What snouts! . . . What an exotic breed!" He planted an orchard, he planted a veritable forest of pines, he experimented with coffee and chicory, and he suddenly decided to plant cabbages in large quantities. He had to have nourishing food for the hogs, and despite his wife's objections, he built a distillery. She felt that this was sinful. They had no overseer. Since he had lost interest in the school, he tried to get one of the student-teachers to undertake the management of the farm. The teacher had no knowledge of farming and gave it up. Then Tolstoy made "an important discovery": "Managers, foremen, and overseers are only a burden on the farm. You can verify this by firing all the overseers, and by sleeping until ten o'clock. You will see that there will be no change for the worse. I have made this experiment and am absolutely convinced." After this "discovery" the management of the estate was divided. The Countess looked after the office, the house, the barns, and the cattle, and paid the hired labor. Tolstoy looked after the fields, the vegetables, the forest, and the bees. To help them, both had several boys who were former pupils of the Yasnaya Polyana school.

The experiment was a failure. The plans seemed sound, but in practice everything went wrong. The Japanese hogs died one after the other, and the reason for it came to light much too late. To look after the hogs, Tolstoy had hired an old overseer who had lost his previous job on account of drunkenness. His new occupation did not appeal to him. Later he confessed, "I would give the hogs as little food as possible to make them weak. It worked! If, the next time I saw them, they were still squeaking, I gave them just a little food. Whenever they became quiet, I knew the end had come."

The hams they sent to sell in Moscow were not properly salted or cured. In warm weather they spoiled and had to be given away. The butter went bad, and green mold appeared around the edges of the wooden casks.

The field work fared no better. A fourteen-year-old boy could not see that his master's orders were carried out on hundreds of acres. Only the young orchard and the young pines thrived.

As a rest after his disappointments, Tolstoy enjoyed shooting. He particularly enjoyed going after snipe in the early spring. At twilight, with his pet setter Dorka, he would stand for hours in the forest listening to the sounds, and to the heavy flight of the birds. He also loved hunting and, forgetting everything and everybody, galloped after his hounds. Once in the autumn of 1864 he took out a thoroughbred English mare for the first time and went alone on a hunt with his borzois. They jumped a hare and the chase was on. The young mare could not clear a deep ditch and fell. Tolstoy dislocated his shoulder and fractured a bone. He remained unconscious for a long time. When he came to, he walked with great difficulty to the main highway and stretched out on the road. Peasants who happened by lifted him onto a wagon and carried him to the nearest village—he told them not to frighten the household. Terrified, the Countess, who was expecting her second child, came running to the village. The doctor who was summoned from Tula could not help him. On the second day they succeeded in finding a surgeon who set his shoulder, but the operation was not successful. Suffering agonies, Tolstoy traveled to Moscow, where his arm was broken again and reset. After a long treatment he was at last able to return to his wife, who had remained with the two children in Yasnaya Polyana. The separation and the worry about each other brought them even closer together and led to a remarkably touching and tender correspondence.

But the earlier letters to his wife, which he wrote during his infrequent absences on hunting expeditions, were filled with amazing passages. In one of them he wrote, "You say that I will forget you. Not for a single minute, and especially when I am with someone else. While I am shooting, I think only of the snipe, but when I am with other people, every thought, every word makes me think of you, and all the time I want to tell you something—something that I can tell only to you."

He believed that, under the influence of his wife, he was becoming an entirely new person. The schools were forgotten. The student-teachers were leaving one by one. As soon as possible he wanted to dispose of his magazine.

On February 8, 1863, he wrote in his diary, "Everything is so clear to me now! It was simply my youth. Nothing more than a bluff, which now that I have grown up I cannot keep up. She is responsible for everything. She has no idea and she cannot understand how much more she has changed me than I have changed her. And she has done it unconsciously. Consciously, both of us are helpless."

During the autumn of the same year he told his friend, Countess Alexandra Tolstoy, about this new Tolstoy who had "grown":

"I am a husband and a father, well pleased with my fate, and so resigned to it that I have to imagine what life would be without all this, in order to realize how happy I am. I no longer search my mind and my feelings. *Grübeln* is forgotten, and in my relations with my wife, I feel instead of thinking. This gives me a wide mental latitude. Never before have I felt my mental and moral capacity so free and so fit for work. I have plenty of work. This work, which has kept me busy since autumn, is a novel about the 1810's and '20's. Is this proof of the weakness of my character, or of its strength? Sometimes I think it is one and sometimes the other. I have to admit that my outlook on life, on people, and on society, is entirely different from the outlook I had when I saw you last. I still pity them, but I cannot understand how I could have loved them so much. But I am glad that I went through the school; it was my last love and it did much to form my mind. I still love children and teaching, but I find it difficult to understand myself as I was a year ago. The children come to see me in the evenings and bring recollections of the teacher that I was, and that I will never be again. Now I am a writer and I write and think as I have never written or thought before. I am a happy, calm husband and father who has no secrets or desires, except a desire that everything may remain as it is now."

In another letter to Countess Alexandra, he wrote:

"You remember I wrote you once saying that people are wrong when they search for a happiness that means no work, no falsehoods, no bitterness, and only serenity and bliss. I was wrong! Such happiness exists; I have known it for the last three years, and each day it becomes deeper and more serene. The material that creates this happiness is not particularly attractive: children who—excuse me—wet themselves and cry; a wife who is nursing one, leading the other by the hand, and constantly accusing me of not being aware that they are on the verge of death; and paper and ink, which are my tools for describing events that have never taken place, and emotions of people who have never existed."

4

Tolstoy's turbulent, many-sided mind could not possibly be absorbed by the management of a farm. After he had calmed down and had rid himself of his obsession for teaching and for the school, he gave himself completely to his creative talent. Now he felt like "an apple tree" that had grown with numerous branches spreading in all directions and which life had pruned, tied, and propped up so it would not interfere with the other trees and would become stronger and grow in a single "trunk." This "trunk" was his creative genius.

Early in 1861, Tolstoy's friends, among them the critic Botkin, thought that he was "unable to write" because his mind was "in a chaos of images"; impatiently they waited for the day when his soul would "settle on something."

They were mistaken. Tolstoy had never stopped writing. He became indifferent to his audience. The spring of his creative force had not run dry; it was merely concealed below the surface of his stormy life. During those years Tolstoy had not published *The Cossacks* or *Polikushka* because they remained in the form of sketches. He seemed not to have enough strength or inspiration to finish them.

His happy love and his marriage supplied the inspiration. His life centered around his family, his wife and his children, and he was anxious to enlarge his income. In 1879, in his *Confession*, he explained what had stimulated his creative activity after his marriage. He wrote, "I had already tasted the temptations of authorship, the temptation of tremendous monetary compensation and of applause in return for a very negligible effort, and I gave in to this temptation so that I could improve my finances and so that I could pacify within me the problems of life in general, and of my own life, which were assailing my soul. I wrote, trying to teach that one should live so that one would be happy within one's own family—the only real truth for me at the time."

Though frank, this statement is hardly just. When he was writing, Tolstoy worked hard. He suffered with his characters and seldom lost sight of the great problems that have to be faced by humanity. But during that period in his life the family was his all-absorbing interest, and marital happiness and family virtues occupy a dominant place in his great novel *War and Peace*. His wife was a living example of domestic virtues, but she also loved fame, artistic creativeness, and wealth. Undoubtedly in this respect their tastes were in accord. At that time the thirty-four-year-old genius had an overwhelming influence on his eighteen-year-old wife. Certainly, if the great writer had changed from a wild apple tree, spreading in all directions, to one neatly pruned, his young wife was not responsible for the change. His sympathies went out to meet the basic tastes of the woman he loved, but of his own accord; though he said that he had been "pruned" by life, he gave himself wholeheartedly and enthusiastically to artistic creation, seeing in it, among other things, a way to fame and wealth.

He had a yearning to write and to write for the public. Before, he had created without publishing. Now he was anxious to sell what he wrote before completing it. A month and a half after his marriage he wanted to begin work on a novel. He wrote to Katkov, the editor of the *Russky Vestnik,* and impatiently waited for an answer. The answer would "decide this matter."

What Katkov answered is not known. Perhaps he reminded him of the advance he had received on *The Cossacks.* In any case, instead of the novel he had been planning, Tolstoy immediately settled down to rework this story, which he had begun in 1852. He delivered it to Katkov on December 19, 1862. Soon after *The Cossacks* Tolstoy finished and published *Polikushka.* He wanted to write so much that, when he was asked for a short play, he produced *The Nihilist* in three days, and it was presented at an amateur performance, with the various parts played by the Countess, Tatyana, and some other relatives.

He wrote a comedy, *The Infected Family,* also on the subject of nihilism, took it to Moscow at once, and was extremely anxious to have the Imperial Theater include it in its repertoire that season. In the autumn of 1863 he was finally at work on the "novel of the 1810's and '20's."

Why had Tolstoy become interested in the military uprising that had taken place on December 14, 1825? Perhaps he had read someone's memoirs; perhaps some stories had been preserved in his family about Prince S. G. Volkonsky, who had taken part in the uprising and who was distantly related to Tolstoy. As soon as he approached the subject, he began analyzing the cause of the political movements of the early part of the nineteenth century. The spirit behind the December Uprising seemed French. So he went further back, to the era of the Napoleonic Wars. That period in Russian history was closely related to the histories of the two families from which he was descended, the Counts Tolstoy and the Princes Volkonsky.

Many of the people who had surrounded Tolstoy in his childhood had been witnesses of the French invasion: his grandmother on his father's side, his father, his aunt, and some of the servants. Later, in the fifties, he met a cousin of his mother's, Princess Volkonsky, who in her youth had often visited the stern general, Prince Volkonsky, and his quiet and resigned daughter, Princess Mary, in Yasnaya Polyana. Musing over the letters and diaries of his relatives, Tolstoy became keenly aware of a warm sense of family, as well as of the problems of war, to which he had already devoted much thought. Gradually his interest shifted from his original theme to the subject of the armed conflict between Russia and Napoleon. Perhaps the scarcity of material on the December Uprising—the archives were closed to the public at that time—was another reason why he abandoned his original project. This was the beginning of the tremendous epic, *War and Peace*. It took five years of Tolstoy's life (1864–69), and involved strenuous and frequently painful work. More than once he had been on the verge of giving it up in despair. When it was finished, it brought him fame and wealth. No other Russian literary masterpiece touches on such a variety of problems of world-wide significance. In *War and Peace* Tolstoy reached the height of patriotic feeling, of family tradition, of love for country life, and of "sane, mediocre ideas." During the early years of his married life he was filled with them, though later, in his search for truth, he came to consider such ideals repulsive and foreign to his mind. The Countess shared his tastes and opinions of that period completely. Undoubtedly these ideals were a part of both of them.

5

Was Tolstoy content with the life of a "pruned, tied, and propped-up apple tree?"

Toward the end of 1865 he discontinued his diary and did not resume it for thirteen years. This might have been due to the strain of his literary work, but he might have had other reasons. The happy married couple had no secrets from each other. Each of them read every word the other wrote and every letter that was received. Under these circumstances, to record frankly in a diary all the tribulations of married life was a difficult matter. Written words could create discords, arouse violent reactions, and produce unexpected complications. Very likely Tolstoy had opportunities to observe that a passing mood, reflected in his diary, tended to grow out of proportion and to become a cloud on the horizon of their family happiness. Perhaps, being unwilling to compromise, or to silence his feelings and thoughts even though they were only of a passing nature, Tolstoy, intolerant of insincerity, was forced to discontinue these talks with himself, which he had continued for so many years.

His infrequent entries about such quarrels as are unavoidable in any family assume a peculiar significance. At first he described them in great detail. These "love wounds" cured with "kiss lotion" upset and embittered him. He knew that "lotion" was the wrong cure. He wrote, "Every quarrel, no matter how trivial, is a love wound. The fleeting emotions of anger, disappointment, pride, and selfishness will pass, but a small scar will remain forever, and will disfigure love—the finest thing in the world." In 1865, along with expressions of his belief that his happiness was "one in a million," brief entries began to appear: "On cool terms with Sonya," or "Something unfriendly between Sonya and me."

More serious doubts appeared.

On June 2, 1863, he wrote, "I thought that I was getting old, that I was dying; I thought that I was afraid, that I no longer loved. I was terrified at myself because I find that my interests center around money and conventional well-being. A recurring period of mental slumber. . . ."

And again:

"How terrible, hateful, senseless to tie one's happiness to material things: wife, children, health, wealth."

In a passing mood he even missed his old "wildness": "Where am I; I, whom I knew and liked, who at times came completely to the surface, and whom I enjoyed and feared? I am small and inconsequential. I have been this way ever since I married the woman I love."

Deep reactions were occurring in his soul. At times they broke through and surprised him.

On January 15, 1863, he wrote, "At home I suddenly growled at Sonya because she would not leave me alone. I felt ashamed and afraid."

In her reminiscences Countess Tolstoy's sister described one of the scenes that took place in 1867:

"Sonya told me that she had been sitting on the floor in her room and going through a drawer of odds and ends. She was expecting a child at the time. Tolstoy entered and said:

" 'Why are you sitting on the floor? Get up!'

" 'I will, as soon as I put these things away.'

" 'I am telling you to get up at once!' he screamed at the top of his voice, turned around, and went to his study.

"Sonya could not understand why he was so angry. She was offended and followed him to his room. From my room I could hear their voices; I listened and could not understand a word. Suddenly I heard something fall, the sound of breaking glass, and Tolstoy shouting:

" 'Get out, get out!'

"I opened the door. Sonya had left. On the floor were pieces of china and a broken thermometer that had been hanging on the wall. Pale, with his lips twitching, Tolstoy stood in the middle of the room. His eyes were fixed on one spot. I felt ashamed and afraid; I had never seen him in such a state. Without saying a word, I ran to Sonya's room. She looked very pitiful. Almost out of her mind, she kept repeating: 'Why? What is wrong with him?' Later she told me:

" 'I went to the study and asked: "What is wrong with you, Lev?"

" 'He screamed angrily: "Get out, get out!" Frightened and surprised, I walked over to him; he held me back with one hand, with the other picked up a tray with a cup of coffee, and threw it on the floor. I tried to catch his hands. He became incensed, tore the thermometer from the wall, and broke it.'

"Sonya and I could never understand the reason for this violent outbreak."

The "pruned, tied" apple tree had suddenly felt its bonds and violently tried to shake them off.

Chapter Five

THE COUNTESS gave birth to her first child on June 28, 1863. Everything went normally, but she had a hard time. The boy was named Sergei. In *Anna Karenina* Tolstoy described what he felt while his first child was being born. Actually, the circumstances were different. The child was born in the country, but a doctor and a midwife had been brought from Tula in time. The Countess's mother and sister were also staying in Yasnaya Polyana.

The child's arrival brought new disagreements. Tolstoy believed that a mother should not only nurse her child but also attend to all its needs without any assistance. The Countess was slow in recovering, the child was restless, and the mother's milk was not satisfactory. The mother-in-law thought that Tolstoy was "making a mess of things," advised him to hire a nurse for the child, and, because her daughter was ill, demanded a wet nurse. The young mother felt ill and became more and more nervous and irritable. Her doctors advised her to discontinue nursing the child. Old Dr. Behrs wrote to Tatyana, "Keep after your restless sister and, as often as you can, warn her against tempting and trying Providence. Give Lev a piece of your mind. Writing and making speeches is one thing, but real life is different. Make him write a story about a husband who tortured his sick wife and forced her to nurse her child; women would stone him to death! Get after him! Demand that he console his wife instead."

Apparently all this depressed Tolstoy. His wife's moods irritated him. He mistrusted the doctors and the people about him, but he was forced to give in: a nurse and a wet nurse appeared in the house. Tolstoy tried his best to stay away from the nursery, and when he came in, he always wore an expression of antagonistic contempt. Soon, however, he became at least partly reconciled. The wet nurse fell ill and had to leave, and the child was fed through a funnel. Tatyana wrote, "On one occasion I remember finding Tolstoy in the nursery trying to quiet the crying child. With a large, trembling hand he was sticking a funnel into the tiny mouth and pouring milk into it."

The family differences and quarrels soon came to an end. Tolstoy had no real reason for complaints. The Countess proved to be an exceptionally good mother.

During the twenty-five years from 1863 to 1888, she bore thirteen children. Three of them died when they were very young, two lived to be five and seven, and the others survived. She nursed almost all of them herself. After the birth of her second daughter, Mary, she was critically ill, and was forced to agree to having in a wet nurse. When she saw her child at the breast of another woman, she became excited and jealous and cried bitterly. Tolstoy considered this jealousy natural and admired his wife's love for her children.

For some time the care of the children created no more discord in the Tolstoy family. When differences arose, the Countess deferred to Tolstoy's extreme demands and in time they were forgotten. For a while the presence of a nurse would upset him, but he became accustomed to it. Later, after he had met and visited Prince Lvov for the first time, he was delighted with the order maintained by an English governess in the Prince's nursery. Tolstoy decided to write to England for her younger sister. Soon the young and energetic Miss Hannah Tursey appeared in Yasnaya Polyana, and the Countess had to carry a dictionary in her pocket and learn to speak English. Tolstoy emphasized simplicity in the training of his children. A boy was expected to be dressed in a thick linen shirt, and a girl in a loose gray flannel blouse. No toys were allowed. When he went to Moscow to buy material for the children's clothes he always chose something fine and expensive—the best he could find.

The English governess promptly introduced her own ideas and tactfully but determinedly insisted on cleanliness and beauty in the life of the children. Without saying much, she gradually changed the children's clothes, and saw that everything was kept spotless by constant washing, scrubbing, and cleaning. She taught the children new games. Tolstoy could not fail to notice the good results of her efforts and was willing to overlook the fact that his original instructions were disregarded.

He was very friendly with his children, especially with his youngest daughter, but he detested kisses, caresses, or any display of tenderness. He always remained at a safe distance from the newly born.

He said, "I cannot hold a little bird in my hands without trembling inwardly, and I am just as afraid to hold a young baby."

Ten years after their marriage, the Tolstoys had six children. In a letter to Countess Alexandra, Tolstoy gave a description of them:

"The eldest [Sergei] is a fair-haired, presentable boy; he has something weak and patient in his expression. His laugh is not infectious, but when he cries I can barely hold back my tears. Everyone says that he very much resembles my eldest brother. I am afraid to believe it—it is too good to be true. . . . Sergei is clever, has a mathematical mind, and is responsive to art; he studies well and he can jump, but he is awkward and absent-minded. He has little originality, and he depends on the physical. He is a different boy when he is well, and when he is sick. Ilya, the second boy, has never been sick; he has large bones, a good color, and he is gay. He is a poor student, always thinks about forbidden subjects, invents his own games. He is neat and careful with his things; the word 'mine' means much to him. He is hot-tempered, violent, and always ready to fight, but at the same time he is gentle and sensitive. He enjoys the pleasures of life and likes to eat and sleep. Everything he does is original. When he cries, he is angry and disagreeable; when he laughs, everybody laughs with him. Anything that is forbidden attracts him and he seeks it out. In the summer, we often went swimming— Sergei on his own horse and Ilya in my saddle. One morning I came out and found them waiting. Ilya, happy and neat, a towel in his hand and a hat on his head, was ready. Sergei, out of breath and without a hat, appeared at the last moment. 'Find your hat or I won't take you!' Sergei looked everywhere but could not find it. There was nothing I could do. 'I won't take you without a hat; this will be a lesson to you. You always lose everything!' He was on the verge of tears. I rode away, expecting Ilya to show some sign of regret. Not at all. He was happy and talked about the horse. My wife found Sergei in tears. She looked for his hat. Finally she guessed that her brother—who had left early that morning to go fishing—had probably worn it. She wrote me a note saying that she thought Sergei was not to blame for losing his hat and she sent him to me in a cap. Incidentally, her guess was correct. I heard quick footsteps on the dock; Sergei was running toward me; he had lost the note on the way and he began to sob. Ilya and I sobbed with him.

"Tatyana is eight years old. Everyone says she is very much like Sonya and, though it is almost too good, I believe it because it is so obvious. If she had been Adam's eldest daughter, and had had no younger children around her, she would have been a terribly unhappy girl. Her greatest joy is to play with the little ones. She seems to experience a physical delight in handling and holding their little bodies. Her dream—which now seems to be quite conscious—is to have children. She is not very clever, she dislikes to work with her mind, but she has a sound mechanism in her head. If God will send her the right husband, she will be a splendid woman. I am willing to give a large reward to the person who will make a happy woman out of her.

"Fourth—Lev. Handsome, graceful, and debonair. His clothes always a perfect fit. He does everything the others do and does it quickly and well. He still cannot understand much.

"Fifth—Mary, two years old—Sonya was very near death with her. She is a weak, sickly child. She has skin as white as milk, light curly hair, and large, strange blue eyes—strange because their expression is deep and serious. She is not pretty, but she is clever. She will be a mystery. She will suffer, she will seek without finding, and she will always reach for the unattainable.

"Sixth—Peter, a giant. A huge, beautiful baby in a bonnet, with elbows sticking out and always on the go. My wife is always delighted, exhilarated, and anxious when she is holding him. I cannot judge him yet. I know that he has a great store of physical strength, but I have no way of knowing whether he has anything for which such physical strength is needed."

The children were growing up. In the early seventies the Tolstoys suddenly felt the problem of education had to be solved. An English governess and a German tutor were no longer adequate. The mechanism that had been running smoothly for several years had suddenly stopped. The children's silent demands were on a higher plane. The Tolstoys had to make a decision; they were loath to move to town until it was absolutely necessary, because giving up their country solitude meant to "spoil everything in our lives, and in the lives of the children." If they were to remain in the country, the education had to be more systematic and the right personnel had to be found. A tireless search began for suitable tutors, teachers, and governesses. Tolstoy assumed all the responsibility in this connection. He corresponded with friends, made trips to Moscow and Tula, and always examined every new applicant thoroughly. He soon assembled a whole staff of Swiss and French tutors, English and Russian governesses and music teachers. The children spent much of their time studying. As in school, they had a regular schedule, and passed from one teacher to another.

The parents took an active part in their education. The Countess taught reading, French, German, and dancing. Tolstoy taught mathematics. Later, when his eldest son reached Greek, and no suitable teacher was available, Tolstoy gave up everything else and set himself to study. Though he did not know even the Greek alphabet when he began, within six weeks he had surmounted the difficulties and was able to read Xenophon and even Homer. Ilya, the third child, has left a description of his father's lessons: "Papa taught me arithmetic. I had listened to the way he had taught Sergei and Tatyana, and I was afraid of those lessons, because when Sergei could not understand something, Papa said that he was being stupid on purpose. A strange expression came into Sergei's eyes and he cried. Sometimes I failed to understand something, and Papa became angry with me. During the early part of a lesson, he was always in a good humor and joked, but later, as it became more difficult, he began explaining, and I became frightened, and could not understand him."

Particular attention was paid to physical training, gymnastics, and exercises intended to develop courage and self-reliance. Tolstoy taught the children to swim. He took them hunting and for long rides on horseback. In the winter, with their help, he made a ring for skating and snow hills for coasting. He skated with them; and for a time he gathered the children every morning in the garden, where he had installed proper equipment, and made them take turns in performing difficult exercises on parallel bars, rings, and a trapeze. Tolstoy had few equals in running, jumping, and gymnastics, and his enthusiasm carried away casual onlookers as well as the children. He was no less enthusiastic about croquet and tennis, the two games that were popular in Yasnaya Polyana. In the evenings he gathered the children together and read aloud to them. Jules Verne's novels were the favorites. If the books had no illustrations, Tolstoy drew the pictures and showed them to the children while he read.

During the first fifteen years of his married life Tolstoy gave a great deal of time and thought to his children. He brought much humor and carefree gaiety into their lives. He knew how to cheer them and how to dispel any gloomy moods. One of the games was known as the gallop of the "Nubian Cavalry." After the departure of some boring guest, the family would remain in the sitting room. The children would cry, quarrel, and squabble. When things would become unbearable, Tolstoy would jump from his chair, lift one hand above his head and, waving it, gallop around the table. The children, imitating his every move, would rush after him. Having circled the room several times, they would flop on their chairs, completely out of breath. The atmosphere would be changed. Everyone would feel refreshed and gay; the quarrels, the boredom, and the tears would be forgotten.

The children had the impression that Mama was the most important person in the house and that everything centered around her. She gave the cook orders about dinner, she gave the children permission to go walking, she sewed their clothes and their underwear, she was always nursing the youngest child, and all day long her quick steps could be heard around the house. Certain liberties could be taken with her, but at times she became angry and strict.

To take liberties with Papa was not advisable. When he looked into anyone's eyes, he could read their thoughts, and no one ever tried to lie to him. Papa never punished anyone, and seldom made the children do things. All, seemingly of their own free will, did the things he wanted them to.

In his reminiscences, Ilya wrote, "Mama scolded and punished us very often. When Papa wanted us to do something, he looked straight at us, and the expression of his eyes was much more eloquent than anything he could have said. This, for instance, illustrates the difference between Father and Mother: We often needed a few pennies for something or other. If I went to Mother, she asked why I needed the money, accused me of being wasteful, and often refused. If I went to Papa, he never asked any questions but looked straight in my eyes and said, 'Take it off the table.' No matter how badly I needed money, I preferred to beg Mother for it rather than go to Father. Father's most important gift as an educator was that no one could hide anything from him any more than he could from his own conscience."

Only their methods differed. As far as their aims in education went, for the first fifteen years they were in complete accord. Their children had to be educated like "other children" of their class. The ancient, patriarchal customs of a wealthy, landed Russian family were firmly rooted in Yasnaya Polyana, and the Tolstoy children's early years were in many ways even happier and more beautiful than the years so warmly pictured in Tolstoy's *Childhood* and *Boyhood*. Their father used his genius to fill the family life with gay energy, love, and good feeling. He was not in the least arbitrary in applying his opinions, convictions, and experience to the children's education. During that period Tolstoy was indifferent to religion. Every evening and every morning the children prayed for their father, their mother, their brothers and sisters, and for all Orthodox Christians. On the eves of important holy days a priest was invited to the house and services were held. The entire family kept the fasts during the first and last weeks in Lent.

Tolstoy was a strong advocate of "free schools" for the people. He believed that a child should be taught only subjects that interested him. But his own children passed from one teacher to another, and were systematically taught the very subjects that made up the official curriculum of the state-supported schools. This was a minimum, from which no one could deviate, and there was no choice.

Tolstoy's eldest daughter, Tatyana, said, "We had five tutors and teachers living in the house, and at least as many more, including a priest, came in from outside to give us lessons. We were taught five or six languages, music, drawing, history, geography, and mathematics, and we had Bible classes."

In 1861 Tolstoy had written about the peasant children, "One cannot describe these children; one has to see them. Among the children who belong to our charming class I have never seen anything like them." Nevertheless, his own children grew up in an atmosphere that was customary among the "charming class."

"We were brought up like gentlemen, proud of our family, and aloof from the rest of the world," wrote one of his sons. "Everything that was not a part of our life was below us, and not worthy of imitation. We had a tendency to look down on the peasant children. I became interested in them when I began to learn from them things I had not known before and which it was forbidden to know. I was then about ten years old. We went to the village during the winter months to coast down the hills and became friendly with several peasant boys, but Papa soon noticed and stopped it. We grew—surrounded by a stone wall of English governesses, tutors, and teachers. Under these circumstances our parents were able to watch every step we made and to guide our lives in accordances with their ideas, especially because they were in complete agreement on our education."

2

"My wife is not playing with dolls. Don't misjudge her that way. To me she is a valuable assistant. . . ."

Thus Tolstoy wrote to Fet in the summer of 1863. He was right. From the very beginning the Countess had tried with all her heart to share her husband's interests. She actively helped him to look after their large and diversified farm, which was operated without the assistance of a manager. She kept the books in the office. Even during the last months of a pregnancy she made the rounds from building to building with a bunch of keys on her belt. When Tolstoy was busy with the apiary, two miles from the house, she brought his lunch to him. She tried, though without much success, to be present in the barn at milking time and to help her husband teach the peasant children.

She even took part in such recreations as hunting and fishing. Tolstoy would choose a narrow spot on the Voronka River, and fasten a net on a long pole. His wife and her sister would walk up the stream and beat the water, driving pike into the net, which Tolstoy would hold—enthusiastic, as always, about what he was doing.

But the wide circle of activities soon narrowed down. The school was closed, and the period of enthusiasm for farming came to an end due to temporary setbacks. The children began to appear and to absorb all of the mother's attention. Complications followed the arrival of the first son: the mother's illness and the growing differences between the parents. In 1864 the arrival of the first daughter was accompanied by another sad experience. Tolstoy, because of a dislocated shoulder, had to spend a month in Moscow, and the Countess, with the two children, could not be with him. The boy was seriously ill, and hovered near death. The young mother was not discouraged and wrote to her husband, "On the contrary, darling, stay in Moscow and don't come back until everything is well here again. At present, you would simply not exist as far as I am concerned, because I am always in the nursery with my restless children. I cannot leave them day or night."

At times the old yearnings reasserted themselves. The child was well again, and Tolstoy, after a successful operation, was expected any day. In the meantime his sister and her children were visiting in Yasnaya Polyana, and long-forgotten music was heard in the house again. The Countess wrote to her husband:

"Music, which I have missed for so long, immediately carried me away from the atmosphere of nursery, diapers, and babies— an atmosphere that I have not been able to leave for a single minute—and brought visions of faraway places where everything is different. I cannot believe that I had silenced in myself these strings that ache and feel at the sound of music or at the sight of nature, so that you could not sense them and were irritated with me. Now I can feel everything and though it hurts me, I like it. We mothers would be better off, if we never felt like this. . . . I look around your study and I remember everything: how before the hunt you were dressing in front of the cupboard with your guns and how Dorka jumped and was impatient, how you sat at the table and wrote, how I opened the door and— afraid to disturb you—peeped inside, and how you, sensing that I was afraid, said, 'Come in.' That was all I wanted. I remember when you were sick, how you lay on the sofa. I remember the painful nights you spent after the accident, Agatha dozing on the floor under the dim lights, and I can never tell you how sad it makes me."

As years went by and the number of children increased, the Countess had more and more to silence the "strings" that she had mentioned in her letter. Less and less often could she allow herself the pleasure of sitting at the piano and playing four-hands with her husband. Tolstoy became aware of her talent for drawing and tried to have a teacher come down from Tula regularly. These aspirations, too, had soon to be abandoned. But the young housewife and mother found other means of expression. She was passionately devoted to the creative talent of her husband, and she found a way to contribute. She took on herself the thankless task of copying his complicated and almost illegible original drafts. She sat at her desk in the drawing room next to the hall and wrote whenever she had time. She spent entire evenings bent over the sheets, deciphering Tolstoy's scrawls, and often she went to bed late at night after everyone else was asleep. When she could not read something, she went to her husband and asked him to decipher it. This happened seldom. She tried not to disturb him. Tolstoy would take the manuscript and in an irritated voice say, "What can't you make out?" He would begin to read but had to pause over the words in question and with great difficulty decipher, or more often guess, what he had written. His handwriting was extremely poor, and he had a habit of writing entire sentences between the lines, in the corners of a page, or even across the face of it. The fresh copies, in the Countess's neat handwriting, came back to Tolstoy to be revised, and when they returned to her again, they were unrecognizable. The same chapter would have to be rewritten and copied several times; some parts were copied five or even ten times. In his reminiscences Stephen Behrs makes the statement that his sister copied out the tremendous novel *War and Peace* seven times.

When the proofs arrived in Yasnaya Polyana, the work would begin all over again. At first only corrections, omitted letters, and stops would be marked in the margins, then occasional words would be changed, then entire sentences, and then entire paragraphs would be taken out and others substituted. When he had finished with them, the proofs looked fairly clean in places and black with corrections in others. They could not be returned because no one but the Countess was able to disentangle the maze of corrections, lines, and words. She would spend another night copying. In the morning a neat stack of pages in her small, precise handwriting would be on her desk, ready to be mailed. Tolstoy would pick them up to look them over "for the last time," and in the evening they would be back again with everything changed and covered with corrections.

"Sonya, darling, excuse me; again I have spoiled your work; I will never do it again," he once said with an apologetic air, showing her the pages. "We will send them off tomorrow."

Often "tomorrow" dragged on for weeks and months.

This Penelopean task never disheartened the Countess. On the contrary, whenever she caught up with her work, she missed it and asked for more. When she sent a manuscript to Moscow, she felt as if she were parting with her own child and was afraid that something would hurt it. In her autobiography she wrote, "Often in copying I was surprised and could not understand why passages that to me seemed so beautiful had been changed or eliminated, and I always rejoiced when they were restored. I was so absorbed in the work of copying, that I frequently sensed the rough spots, such as an excessive use of the same word or a long sentence in which punctuation had to be changed to bring out the thought more clearly. I called my husband's attention to them. Sometimes my comments delighted him, or else he explained why he had to do it that way, and said that details were not important, and only the general effect counted. . . . In copying, I at times took it on myself to call his attention to, and even ask him to eliminate, anything that seemed unfit to be read by young people. For example, the scenes in *War and Peace* built around the cynical and beautiful Helen—and Lev often agreed. Frequently, as I copied the beautiful poetical passages in my husband's writings, I cried, not only because I was moved, but also from artistic exaltation that I shared with the author."

Gradually the girl who had been thinking the thoughts and repeating the words of her husband began to show signs of independence. She made a number of improvements in the appearance of the house and in the routine of the household. Tolstoy grumbled at this display of energy. He disliked anything new.

She took the leather pillow that he had been using and replaced it with a feather pillow covered with silk and enclosed in a pillowcase. Self-consciously she said, "Lev, you will be more comfortable with this one."

The weeds and thistles around the house depressed her. After hesitating for a long time, she gave the servants orders to clear away the rubbish around the house, bring gravel for the walks, dig flower beds, and plant flowers.

Tolstoy grumbled, "Why is this necessary? We lived well enough without it."

But he followed her example and gave orders to have the benches painted and the paths in the garden swept.

Without being urged, he solved the difficult problem of supplying the house with good drinking water by having it brought from the Voronka River, over a mile away. The Countess gradually took over all the household cares, changed the routine, and surrounded her husband with the comforts that meant so much to him almost until his last day. On one occasion Sologub, the well-known writer, visited Yasnaya Polyana. After watching the young married couple, he said to the Countess, "You are a regular nurse caring for your husband's talent, and I hope you will continue this work for the rest of your life."

After *War and Peace* was finished, Tolstoy returned to his enthusiasm for educational work. Without giving up creative writing entirely, and working from time to time on two historical novels, *December Uprising* and *Peter I,* he devoted most of his time to the development of an educational theory based on his practical experiences. He published two primers that illustrated his ideas of the best method of teaching reading. By then, he was already so widely known that his attack on the generally accepted methods could not remain unnoticed. An interchange of opinions followed, which grew particularly lively after Tolstoy's violent article "On Public Education" appeared in the best-known periodical of the day, *Otechestvinni Zapiski.* This article created a furor. Plunging ahead with his new enthusiasm, Tolstoy was not satisfied with writing articles. He appeared in person before the Committee on Education in Moscow, defended his

method, and even won a contest in the two parallel schools operated by the Committee on Education—one in accordance with
Tolstoy's word-building method, the other in accordance with
the standard method. He invited teachers from near-by schools
to Yasnaya Polyana and held classes and discussions for them.
He dreamed and worked to organize a "village university"—an
institution of higher learning where the more gifted among the
peasant children could continue their education without giving
up their mode of life. In order to test his theories, early in 1872
Tolstoy again opened a school for peasant children in Yasnaya
Polyana, and invited his entire family and his guests to take part
in the work. The Countess wrote:

"After the holidays we decided to organize a school and now
about thirty-five children come here every afternoon and we
teach them. We all teach: Sergei, Tatyana, Uncle Kostya, Lev,
and I. Teaching ten children at the same time is difficult but it
is interesting and gay. We have divided the pupils among us and
I took eight boys and two girls. Sergei and Tatyana do their work
well. Within a week their pupils have learned the letters and can
build words. As classrooms we use the hall (which is a huge
room), the small dining room, and the new study. The reason
why we are doing this is because ability to read is so important
and because the children are so eager and willing to study."

The school lasted only a short time, but the enthusiasm for
educational matters continued and gradually began to puzzle the
Countess. Toward the end of the year a critical note can be dis-
cerned in her letters: "In that house we have a crowd of public-
school teachers, about twelve of them, who have come here for
a week. Lev is showing them his methods of teaching children to
read, and they are discussing them. Children who have never
been in school have been brought here, and the problem is how
long it will take them to learn according to Lev's methods. The
novel has been forgotten and I am very much disappointed."

This disappointment lasted for some time. Toward the end of
1874 the Countess wrote to her brother, "Our serious winter life
is settling into a routine. Lev is interested only in public educa-

tion, schcols, teachers' schools—that is, schools where public-
school teachers will be taught—and this takes up his entire time
from morning until night. I look at it with amazement. I am
sorry he is spending his strength on this work instead of on writing a novel. I cannot understand how this can be so important if
all the activities are confined to such a small corner of Russia,
Krapivensky County."

At last she openly expressed her thoughts in a letter: "Lev has
decided to write another A-B-C, similar to the American first,
second, and third readers. . . . The novel is not progressing, and
we are flooded with letters from the editors offering ten thousand
advances and five hundred for every page. Lev refuses even to
mention them, as if he were not in the least concerned. Money
makes no difference to me. The important thing is the work itself—the writing of novels. I love it, and it exhilarates me, but
I despise these A-B-C's, arithmetics, and grammars, and I cannot
pretend that I am interested in them. Now something is lacking
in my life, something I love, and that something is Lev's work,
from which I have always derived so much pleasure, and for
which I have such deep admiration."

Gradually, after twelve years of married life, differences began
to arise between them. The young wife already had her own
tastes and thoughts, and she was not afraid to express them in
an open and direct manner.

In this instance everything ended happily. The novel mentioned in her letter was *Anna Karenina*. Begun on March 19,
1873, and written with long interruptions, it was finished in
1877, and became one of the cornerstones of Russian literature.
Tolstoy's preceding literary experiments—*December Uprising*
and *Peter I*—remained in the form of sketches, but *Anna
Karenina* brought back the happy days when the Countess sacrificed hours of sleep in order to decipher and copy the hopelessly
entangled pages of Tolstoy's manuscripts.

3

War and Peace was quickly sold out. By popular demand a second edition was printed. The critics were divided. Some praised it without reservation, others found many shortcomings. The fate of some works of art is above criticism. Tolstoy's novel was one that attained this height. The reading public immediately embraced the novel, which—in addition to its literary qualities—had so many things dear to the Russian heart. *War and Peace* soon became, and thereafter remained, the national Russian epic. After its publication general opinion conceded Tolstoy the first place among contemporary Russian writers. Tolstoy's ventures in the field of education added to his wide popularity. Twelve years before, with all his usual enthusiasm, he had worked in his school and had written thought-provoking articles in his magazine, *Yasnaya Polyana,* expressing his ideas, which were diametrically opposed to the accepted Russian-German methods of education. All this had proved of no avail. Now, in the seventies, Tolstoy's articles in periodicals and his appearances at debates attracted everyone's attention. Teachers were not alone in discussing his ideas on public education. Every paper and magazine joined in the discussion. The attention of the thinking public was centered on Tolstoy. His primers failed to receive the approval of the government; consequently, they could not be used in public schools, and some time elapsed before they won the place they deserved. His first *A-B-C* and the parallel *First Reader*—which were quite expensive—became valuable items for book collectors. Within twenty-five years one and a half million copies of his second *A-B-C* were sold.

The appearance of *Anna Karenina* was a major event. The copies of the *Russky Vestnik* in which *Anna Karenina* had appeared in installments for several years were in great demand. They were read with equal eagerness in the salon of the Empress and in the homes of all classes. In many ways the novel ran contrary to the fashionable ideas of the day. The radically inclined critics tried to dampen the public enthusiasm by pointing out what they termed the reactionary background of the novel. But Tolstoy had taken the public by storm: he stood above fashion. His position as dean of Russian writers was confirmed, and forever after firmly secured for him. Not all the ideas expressed in the novel suited Dostoyevsky, yet he was enthusiastic about it. In the *Journal of an Author* for the year 1877 he quotes the opinion of "an outstanding Russian novelist" about *Anna Karenina*—calling it "an opinion which I share in its entirety":

"It is unheard of—an event of the first importance. Who among our writers can be compared with him? And in Europe, who has created anything that approaches it? Have they ever had anything in their literature that can be called its equal?"

This was real, indisputable, lasting fame. He could not look for anything more in that field.

With fame came money. Farming at Yasnaya Polyana brought no income, but Tolstoy had another farm about a hundred miles from there, Nikolskoye, which he had inherited from his elder brother in 1860. Nikolskoye was within the black-earth belt and, without any effort, was made to bring in about five thousand rubles a year. The family lived on this money and even found it possible to spend an occasional month or two in Moscow. When his income was substantially increased by the sales of *War and Peace,* Tolstoy decided to invest it by extending his land holdings. He began to look for suitable land and in 1869 undertook an extensive journey through the Province of Penza in an attempt to buy land profitably in that wilderness. He could not find anything, but he continued to look in other sections that he considered reasonable and among them the steppes around Samara. He had taken a rest cure there before his marriage and he was familiar with the country.

In 1871 Tolstoy was as ill as he had been ten years earlier. "A generally run-down condition. . . . I need and want nothing except rest, which I cannot find," he diagnosed his illness. The Countess was convinced that his ill health was a result of overwork. Just before his breakdown, Tolstoy—with his usual enthusiasm—had begun to study Greek and to read the classics. "God has afflicted me with this foolishness," he wrote, and he was happy in it. But his wife refused to share his enthusiasm and saw in it only the cause of her husband's illness. He had to recuperate. After several consultations with Moscow doctors, Tolstoy decided to take a rest cure and to visit the places in the Province of Samara where he had been ten years before. During the six weeks of his absence, Tolstoy found time to write his wife fourteen letters filled "with more than love." In one he wrote, "Each day I spend away from you I worry and think about you more vividly and passionately, and it is difficult for me. I cannot talk about it . . ." And again: "I cannot read your letters without tears. I tremble and my heart races. You write whatever comes into your head, but to me every word is full of meaning and I read them over and over."

The rest brought back Tolstoy's strength and his capacity to enjoy life. He found in the virgin Samara steppes a suitable tract of land of about twenty-seven hundred acres, at the ridiculous price of seven rubles an acre. He wrote to his wife, "This purchase is an unbelievably good buy. . . . Compared with Yasnaya Polyana the return from the land here is ten times greater, while the effort spent is ten times less." The transaction was completed in 1872. Tolstoy went to his new estate, to begin building and to break the ground. The following summer the entire family went to the Samara steppes. Tolstoy's hopes of large profits from the exploitation of the newly acquired land failed to materialize. The black earth around Samara is dependent upon rainfall, and a drought brings in its wake a disastrous crop failure. Between 1871 and 1873 the entire district was in distress. The Bashkirs and the Russian peasants had used all their grain reserves, and the new crops were insufficient to tide them over. A famine was threatening. Tolstoy could not be indifferent to a calamity that had befallen the people around him. Generously and in many different ways he helped the Bashkirs and the peasants in his district. The Countess insisted that she persuaded him "to consider this problem seriously." He conducted a regular survey. As a result of his inquiries, a letter telling of the threatening famine and signed by him appeared in the *Moskovski Vedomosti*: "The disaster is here already and one cannot look calmly at the people. And this is only summer: the disastrous year has just begun; the new crop is twelve months away, and opportunities still exist to earn money in other ways, which will temporarily save them from starvation. . . ."

Tolstoy had no faith that the local government representatives would take the situation seriously. He wrote to his cousin at court, asking her to secure a donation from the Empress. Tolstoy's work had important results. All over Russia contributions were made, totaling almost two million rubles, and the government centered its attention on the plight of the district.

Though he had bought the land at a bad time, and returns were poor, Tolstoy continued the work on his new estate. He and his entire family spent several more summers in Samara. In 1878 he added several thousand more acres to his estate, at thirteen rubles an acre. He tried to breed horses and at one time had a herd of four hundred head. Like his other undertakings, the new venture was not a success and was gradually reduced in scale.

In the late seventies Tolstoy quite obviously had no reason to worry about money. Though he had a large family, which never lacked anything essential, through his literary efforts he had succeeded in enlarging his capital considerably. In the early eighties he estimated that he was worth about six hundred thousand rubles.

All the elements of "good, honest happiness," as Tolstoy understood it then, were in evidence: fame such as had never been enjoyed by any other living Russian writer, adequate financial means, and a charming, friendly, gay family.

They knew how to enjoy life in Yasnaya Polyana.

Tolstoy rose quite late, came out of the bedroom in a bathrobe and, with his beard tangled and uncombed, went to dress downstairs in his study. He emerged, dressed in a gray shirt and feeling energetic and refreshed, and went into the dining room to drink tea. The children were already eating their lunch. When no guests were present, he never lingered in the dining room. Carrying a glass of tea, he went back to his study. If there were guests, he engaged them in conversation, became animated, and could not leave. With one hand stuck in his leather belt and with a full glass of tea in the other, he stood by the door for hours, talking with glee and animation. At last he went to work. In winter the children ran to their classes and in summer into the garden to play tennis or croquet, or to swing on the giant's ride. The Countess settled in the drawing room to sew clothes for one of the children or to finish copying a manuscript that she had not had time to get through the night before. Peasant men and women, with their children, frequently came to her with their ills; she talked to them, tried to help them, and distributed, free of charge, standard medicines, which she kept in the house. Until three or four in the afternoon complete quiet reigned in the house. "Lev is at work!" Then he came out of his study, went for a walk or a swim. Sometimes he went with a gun and a dog, sometimes on horseback, sometimes on foot. At five the bell in front of the house was rung. The children ran to wash their hands. Everybody gathered for dinner. Very often Tolstoy was late. He came in much embarrassed, apologized to his wife, and poured himself a silver whisky glass full of homemade brandy. Usually he was hungry and ate anything that was already on the table. The Countess tried to restrain him and asked him not to eat so much cereal because the meat and vegetables were still to come.

"Your liver will bother you again!"

He never listened and kept asking for more until he had his fill.

With great animation he recounted his impressions of the afternoon. Everyone enjoyed them. He joked with the children and with anyone at the table, and no one could resist his gay mood. After dinner he worked in his study again, and at eight the entire family gathered around the samovar. They talked, read aloud, played, sang, and very often the children who were in the same room were included. For the children the day ended at ten o'clock, but voices could be heard in the drawing room until much later. Cards and chess were always popular, and so were endless arguments. Tolstoy sat at the piano and the Countess played four-hands with him, trying desperately to keep time. Occasionally her sister Tatyana sang for them. After several involved and heartbreaking affairs, she had married a friend of her childhood days—her cousin Kuzminsky—in 1868, and with her husband and children, she spent almost every summer with the Tolstoys. Summer in Yasnaya Polyana was a continuous round of festivities. Their relatives were irresistibly attracted by the charming family. In addition to the Kuzminskys other members of the Behrs family came for long visits; as well as Lev's sister, Countess Mary Tolstoy, with her children; Count Sergei Tolstoy, and the Dyakov family, Fet and many others also dropped in for a few days.

All the care in connection with the sleeping arrangements and food for this large crowd fell entirely on the Countess. Family celebrations and reunions, in winter as well as in summer, at times made her task almost unbearable. In January, 1865, she wrote, "We decided to have a ball and a masquerade. . . . You never saw such preparations—the entire household is upside down. Lev and I built the throne. . . . Barbara was dressed as a page. . . . Elizabeth was dressed as an Algerian. . . . Lev dressed the dog, Dushka, as a retired major. . . . The day laborer was dressed as a wet nurse and he carried in his arms Vasily Belka, the cook's son, who wore a diaper. With the help of two other people, we made a hobbyhorse and let Dushka ride it. We were ready, it was after six, but Sergei still had not arrived. We were about to give up hope, when we heard bells and Sergei appeared with a crowd of people, a trunk, and all sorts of baggage. They were taken to my bedroom, where they dressed. Lev dressed his friends in his study. Mary had her friends use her room. I was looking after the lights, the food, and the children. . . . The musicians arrived . . . the music began, the doors were opened and the couples marched in. A midget dressed as a devil led the procession and Sergei's couples followed. . . . Bells, noise, firecrackers, rattles, and at the tail end of the procession, a giant who almost reached the ceiling and looked very natural. . . . I cannot begin to describe the effect. All the servants crowded into the room. . . . You cannot imagine the chaos! Songs, dances, firecrackers, balloon fights, hide-and-seek, ring-around-a-rosy, refreshments, and last of all, fireworks. . . . I spent most of the time downstairs with the children and I must confess that the uproar tired me. Endless days of worrying about dinners, suppers, beds, refreshments, and so forth. The feast lasted until three o'clock. Everyone spent the next day with us. We went riding in two troikas and had an exciting race."

In 1871 an addition had to be built to the house. To celebrate its completion, another masquerade was held during the Christmas holidays, very much like the one described. Among other maskers a wandering actor appeared with two trained bears and a goat. The wandering actor was Tolstoy's friend Dyakov, two relatives were the bears, and Tolstoy was the goat.

Christmas was always a time for a celebration. Long in advance the entire family began to prepare Christmas-tree decorations and presents for the peasant children.

Occasionally a celebration was less noisy and more moving. Mrs. Kuzminsky described a formal dinner on the Countess's name day:

"On the seventeenth of September. Everyone, including myself, was in a festive mood. We wore light dresses with colored ribbons. The dinner table was decorated with flowers and the new porch was flooded with sunlight. I remember how noisy and gay we were, as at five o'clock we took our places at the table. Suddenly music reached our ears from the garden. The band was playing Sonya's favorite—the overture to the opera *Fenella, the Mute of Portici*. Everyone except Sonya knew that Tolstoy had asked the Colonel to send the regimental band, but we had kept the secret. Sonya's expression was beyond description! Everything was reflected there: surprise, fear that it was a dream, joy, and a tenderness when she looked at Tolstoy's face and understood. He was as delighted as she was."

Tolstoy amazed people by the intensity of feeling he displayed for his young wife. He even learned to play the guitar, and sang: "Tell her that with my fiery soul . . ."

These were their happy days. In 1872 Tolstoy wrote to his cousin, "My life goes on in the same way. I could not ask for anything better."

Chapter Six

IN THE midst of this carefree happiness, sad and heavy thoughts took sudden possession of Tolstoy—thoughts of death.

As early as 1863 he wrote, "I am sliding—sliding down the hill of death—and I can barely find strength to stop. I have no desire to die. I love and I yearn for eternal life."

His letters and diaries of the sixties and seventies are filled with similar remarks.

As time went on, these thoughts appeared more often. They became deeper and acquired a hold on him. His reading also drove him in this direction.

In 1869 he asked Fet, "Have you any idea what this summer meant to me? A boundless admiration for Schopenhauer and a spiritual satisfaction that I have never experienced before. I have ordered all his books and I am reading them. (Also, I have been reading Kant.) I doubt that any student taking his course has ever studied any harder or learned more than I have during this summer. Maybe some day I shall change my mind, but now I am convinced that Schopenhauer is the greatest genius ever produced by the human race."

Tolstoy was drawn to people who, though "they have a wholesome outlook on life," always stand on its edge and see it clearly because they look at intervals into Nirvana, into eternity, into the unknown, into Sarsar. He believed that looking into Nirvana strengthened a man's power to see. He wanted to analyze life, to go mentally beyond its limitations.

Because of Tolstoy's exceptionally vivid imagination such experiments were certain to leave their mark on him. He was still interested in worldly affairs, but an occasional glimpse of Nirvana at times filled his heart with cold terror.

2

Toward the end of August, 1869, Tolstoy learned that an estate was for sale at a reasonable price in the wilderness of the Province of Penza. He journeyed there with his manservant, Sergei. From Nizhnii Novgorod they had to travel about three hundred miles with post horses. On the way they spent a night in the small town of Arzamas. In Arzamas he unexpectedly went through a harrowing experience.

At the next stop he wrote to his wife, "Has anything happened to you or to the children? For the second day I am assailed with worry. Two nights ago I was in Arzamas and something strange happened. At two o'clock in the morning I was terribly tired, I wanted to sleep and I had no pains. Suddenly misery, fear, and terror, such as I have never experienced before, gripped me. I will tell you in detail about them later, but I have never felt such a tormenting sensation and I hope God will spare anyone else from it. I jumped out of bed and gave orders to harness the horses. While they were getting them ready, I fell asleep and when I awoke I was entirely well. In a much weaker form I had the same sensation yesterday while we were driving, but I was prepared for it and I refused to give in. At present I am as healthy and as gay as I can be without my family. During this absence I have realized for the first time how much you and the children are a part of my life. I can be myself while I am at work as I am in Moscow, but when I have nothing to do I feel that I simply cannot be alone."

No one knows the details of his experience, which Tolstoy described to his wife when he saw her. Fifteen years later he wrote a story, *Diary of a Madman,* which was published posthumously. This story is unquestionably autobiographical. The chief character is traveling to the Province of Penza to buy a country estate. His manservant, Sergei, is with him. From Nizhnii Novgorod they travel on horseback. They stop at Arzamas for the night. Tolstoy describes the awakening:

"I felt that I could not go to sleep. Why had I come here? Where am I going? What and how am I escaping? I am trying to escape something terrible, which I cannot escape. I am always with myself and I am the tormentor. I—that is it!—I am here. A country estate in Penza or anywhere else will not add anything to me or take anything from me. I am the one who has tired myself, who is unbearable, insufferable to myself. I want to fall asleep, to forget myself, and I cannot. I cannot escape myself.

"I went out into the hall. Sergei was sleeping on a narrow bench, his arm dangling in the air, but he was sleeping soundly. The watchman with a spot on his face was asleep too. I went out into the hall, hoping that I should escape my tormentor, but he followed me and obscured everything. I was terrified. What kind of stupidity is this? Why all this misery, what am I afraid of?

" 'Of me,' inaudibly answered the voice of death. 'I am here!' I felt goose pimples all over my body. Yes, of death. She will come, she is here, and she should not be. If I were actually facing death, I could not possibly suffer more than I am suffering now. I should be frightened, but now I felt more than fear. I saw, I felt approaching death, and at the same time I felt that it could not be here. My entire being felt a yearning, a right to live, and it was also conscious of the act of death that was taking place. This internal tearing was terrifying. I tried to rid myself of the horror. I found a brass candlestick with a piece of a candle in it and lighted it. The red flame and its size—just slightly shorter than the candlestick—kept saying: Death is the only thing in life that should not be. I tried to think about my affairs, about the estate, about my wife. I could not find anything to console me. Everything had turned to nothingness. The horror of my receding life was overshadowing everything else. I had to sleep. As soon as I stretched out, I was up—more horrified than ever. Misery, misery—the same misery of the soul that one feels when an illness is coming on, except that now the soul was having the pains. I am frightened. I am terrified. Apparently I am afraid of death, but when I remember my life, I am afraid of the receding life. Somehow life and death are blended into one. Something is trying to tear my soul apart, and is not strong enough. Once again I went to look at the sleeping men. Once again I tried to sleep. And still the same red, white, square horror. Something is trying to break, and cannot break. Torment—dry, angry torment. I have no feeling of kindness in me, only hatred—calm, even hatred—of myself and of that which has created me."

Though he had lost his faith long before, he tried to pray, but to no avail. At last, in the fresh air, riding in the company of other men, he escaped from his misery. But he felt that something new remained in his soul and poisoned his life.

Apparently the experience, the details of which Tolstoy had promised to tell his wife, was a vivid vision of death. Forever after it was known in the family as the "Arzamas misery." At the time he believed that the vision had passed without leaving any traces: the apparition of death had intruded on Tolstoy's happy life and had disappeared. Everything was as it had been before. Once again Tolstoy was gay and full of energy. But the very power of his imagination carried with it the danger of a reaction from such an experience. He felt the threat and took steps to guard against it. At home he was immune to the "Arzamas misery" for a long time. When he went away, he always took along a member of his family. But away from home the attacks continued to occur. Veiled hints of them here and there in his diaries, but evidently they were not as acute as the one described in the story. They were more like passing moods, like sad thoughts about the futility of things, mere interruptions in his gay and happy life. The emotional mental picture of death which had shocked Tolstoy in Arzamas was absent. As soon as the passing moods left him, he was happy and could not ask for anything better.

But death had not forgotten Tolstoy. On November 9, 1873, after eleven years of happy life, death struck the family for the first time. His year-and-a-half-old son, Peter, died. The Countess was desolate. She wrote, "I believe he did not suffer much. He slept a great deal during his illness and nothing horrible happened—no convulsions, no tortures, and I thank God for that. I even consider it a grace that the youngest died instead of one of the older ones, but I cannot conceal how much I feel this loss. . . . Ten days have gone by and still I am lost, still I am waiting to hear his steps and his tiny voice calling me from a distance. None of the children ever were more attached to me, none ever shone with as much gaiety and kindness. Whenever I felt sad, whenever I had a minute of rest after teaching the children, I played with him. . . . And now everything is the same, but all the joy and all the gaiety in life are gone. . . . Our life goes on as of old, and only for me the happy light in our home has been extinguished—the light that the gay, lovable Peter gave me and which brightened my sad moments."

On June 20, 1874, Tolstoy's old "Aunt," Tatyana Yergolsky, died. Tolstoy wrote, "Two days ago we buried Aunt Tatyana. She had been dying slowly and by degrees and I became accustomed to the thought, but her death, as the death of anyone near and dear, was an entirely new, distinct, and unexpectedly shocking experience."

Another eight months, and on a stormy February day the Tolstoys were again at the cemetery. After three agonizing weeks they had lost their ten-months-old son Nicholas.

Toward the end of the same year the Tolstoy children had whooping cough. In nursing them, the Countess contracted the disease and during an attack gave premature birth to a girl, who lived only a few days. The mother also hovered on the brink of death.

Another month—the end of December, 1875—and Tolstoy's aunt, Pelageya Yushkova, who had just moved from a convent to Yasnaya Polyana, died. She was the aunt in whose home in Kazan Tolstoy had spent his youth. Tolstoy attached a special significance to her death, which had been unusually painful. Though he had never been very close to her, he insisted that her death had an effect on him which no other death had ever had before.

These five deaths within two years made a deep impression on him. At regular intervals someone seemed to knock persistently at Tolstoy's soul and remind him of the world beyond.

Through all this period the Countess was seriously ill. She lost weight and had a continuous cough and severe pains in her back. Embittered and sick, she wrote, "Lev's novel—*Anna Karenina* —has just appeared, and is meeting with great success. My feelings are so mixed. We have had so much unhappiness in our home, and everyone is congratulating us."

Tolstoy's reactions were deeper and more significant. He said that beginning with the years 1874–75, he began to experience more and more frequently the "stops" in life. In the midst of his daily activities he suddenly stopped and asked himself, "What for? What will come next?" He felt that he could not work or live without knowing why. He was interested in his estate in the Samara steppes, and suddenly a question arose in his mind: "What if I have six thousand acres and three hundred head of horses in Samara? What does it matter? What will come next?" He could not find any answer.

During a discussion of the needs of the peasants he suddenly asked himself, "What concern is it of mine?"

Thinking about his literary fame, he said to himself, "What if my fame should be greater than the fame of Gogol, or Pushkin, or Shakespeare, or Molière, or of all the writers on earth? What does it matter?" In the face of approaching, inevitable death he could not find an answer.

He thought, "No matter how important my affairs may seem, they will be forgotten and I shall be no more. Then why should I toil? What surprises me is that man can be blind enough to live! A person can live only while he is intoxicated with life. When he becomes sober, he cannot help seeing that everything is deceit—a stupid deceit! Not even amusing or clever—just cruel and stupid!"

His imagination was too strong and his horror of eternal darkness—of death—too great. Strangely enough, he often thought of suicide as a means of escape. He—a happy man—hid a rope from himself, so that he would not hang himself between two cupboards in the room where he undressed every evening. He stopped going hunting with a gun, so that he would not be tempted to end his life so easily.

Fifteen years earlier Tolstoy had experienced the first revulsion from life. It came after the death of his favorite brother. "A stone cannot be made to fall upward when forces draw it downward. One cannot laugh at a boring joke. One cannot eat without an appetite. What does anything matter, if tomorrow the pains of death with all their disgusting lies and self-deceptions will lead one toward nothingness, toward a zero for oneself?"

Then he was still full of vigor. Thirst for work, for fame, for personal happiness had soon asserted themselves, and he had again been swallowed by the vortex of life.

Now he was different. He was nearing fifty. He felt that he had experienced and tasted everything. He had "a kind, loving, and beloved wife, good children, and a large estate, which was growing and prospering" without any effort on his part. He was more respected than ever before by his relatives and friends. Everyone praised him, and without conceit, he could consider himself famous.

Such was his own conception of himself. In reality, his achievements were much greater. He had gained everything he sought in life. His fame, his material well-being, and his personal happiness left nothing to be desired.

Now everything seemed less enticing than it had before. His power of imagination allowed Tolstoy to enjoy pleasures only while he was seeking them. A layer of surfeit settled over his happy life.

Even then, if a sorceress had appeared and had asked him what he wanted, as of old, he could have answered, "Let everything be as it is!" But that was the very promise the sorceress could not have made. The stormy growth of his strength was at an end. The future held only a decline, a weakening of physical and mental powers, and illnesses, with death just beyond the horizon.

Tolstoy wanted eternity. Could the sorceress promise it to

him? Only recently he had hoped to deepen his understanding of life by concentrating his thoughts on death.

In the cold light of approaching Nirvana the void, the futility of violent Sarsar were revealed.

What was the sense of human existence if Tolstoy, his fame, and his family were to turn into nothing?

His thoughts and his constant excursions into the fields of science and philosophy seemed to lead him to an indisputable conclusion: human life was senseless. Essentially, his attacks of melancholy were a result not only of his fear of death, but of his horror before the senselessness of a life that culminated in death.

These attacks continued to recur, and again and again his soul seemed torn from his body. In the *Diary of a Madman* he wrote, "I lived, I live, and I must live, and then suddenly comes death and the destruction of everything. What, then, is the purpose of life? Is it death? Should I kill myself now? I am too much of a coward. Should I wait for death to come? I fear it even more that way. I would have to live. What for? So I could die?"

Toward the end of 1876 the Countess wrote, "Lev persists in saying that everything is at an end—that death is not far away, that he can enjoy nothing, and that he can expect nothing from life."

One detail is typical of his mood during those difficult days: *Anna Karenina* has two hundred and thirty-nine chapters. Only one of them has a title—the twentieth chapter of the fifth part. And it is called "Death."

3

"How can I save myself? I feel that I am perishing. I live and I am dying, I love life and I am afraid of death—how can I save myself?"

That is Tolstoy's description of his state of mind in June, 1878.

His *Confession* unfolds in vivid detail a picture of the psychological process that made him seek salvation in religion.

He looked at the educated people who belonged to his social stratum. Most of them were agnostics. Among them he could not hope to find an answer to the question that tormented him.

He saw people who could not understand the problem at all, or who answered it with intoxication with life, or who had understood and had committed suicide, or who had understood and were dragging through their hopeless lives out of weakness.

The people of his social class who believed were not any better. They lived amid plenty and tried to hold and increase their wealth. They were afraid of privations, of suffering, and of death. They satisfied their desires and lived as badly as the agnostics, if not worse.

Tolstoy found his salvation in idealizing the life of the "working people." He believed that these people had not avoided the question that tormented him and had "answered it with amazing clarity." Regardless of privations, "they are satisfied with life. They live, suffer, and accept death calmly, even joyfully." They were deprived of almost all the pleasures of life, yet they were happy.

These naïve conclusions put his mind at rest. He decided to accept from the plain people their sturdy and confident outlook on life and death. He listened to what the peasants had to say about God, about faith, about life, about salvation, and he felt that a knowledge of faith was being opened to him, and that he "understood the truth more and more clearly." His friend Strakhov described how Tolstoy once led him out on the highway about a quarter of a mile from the house. They met some men and women who were on a pilgrimage. "They talked with us and told us some remarkable tales. About two miles farther were two small villages where pilgrims were taken in for the night, not for profit, but for 'the soul's salvation.' . . . Eight old men and women were staying in one house and every one of them was doing what he or she pleased. Some were praying, others eating supper, still others resting. Invariably somebody was talking, relating his experiences, explaining. . . . I listened with a great deal of interest."

What could the Russian peasants, the pilgrims, and the wanderers teach Tolstoy?

Here is how he described the purpose attributed to life by the Russian working people: "Every man in this world was created through the will of God. God has created man so that every man can save or destroy his soul. The purpose of every man's life is to save his soul. In order to save it, a man must live in accordance with God's will, and God's will is that a man deny himself the pleasures of life, that he work, resign himself to his fate, suffer, and be kind."

Tolstoy was delighted with this interpretation of life, which he believed was derived by the people from the Christian teachings, as presented by the legends, dogmas, and rituals of the Orthodox Eastern church. A man had to refuse this conception of the purpose of life, or he had to accept it with all its attributes: sacraments, rituals, fasts, and the worship of relics and icons.

Tolstoy seemed not to care how strange some of the ingredients were that went to make up the faith of the people. He accepted it in its entirety. He attended services, he stood while he prayed in the mornings, and in the evenings he fasted and went to confession. At first his mind showed no signs of rebellion. At any cost he had to find a purpose in life which could not be destroyed by death. He believed that he had found it at last and he shut his eyes to everything else.

Twenty years earlier the purpose of life had not seemed to Tolstoy in any way connected with religion. In explaining his reasons for writing the story *Three Deaths* (1858), he had said, "A peasant dies calmly because he is not a Christian. He performs the rituals as a matter of course, but his true religion is different. His religion is nature, with which he lived. He cuts down trees, he sows and reaps, he butchers sheep, and sees new sheep born. He watches as children are born and old men die, and he steadfastly knows the law, which he makes no effort to avoid. . . . He faces it simply and openly."

Whatever his opinion had been then, in the late seventies Tolstoy was certain that the peasant's conception of the world, which had attracted him, was based on the Orthodox faith, and he was willing to accept it because, as he said, he had "nowhere else to go."

The first indication of Tolstoy's interest in religion can be found in the last pages of *Anna Karenina*. Reading them, Dostoyevsky questioned the soundness of the faith that Levin acquires from the peasants. He thought it could not be a final faith. He even doubted that a person like Levin could have a final faith. Dostoyevsky wrote, "No matter how much he tries, he will always retain in his soul a shade of what, I believe, can be called aimless wandering—a physical and spiritual aimlessness—which, no matter how he struggles to overcome it, will always remain a part of his heritage. . . . His faith will be destroyed again by himself; it will not be long before some new offshoot will appear, and all at once the entire structure will collapse."

Dostoyevsky's predictions came true.

Tolstoy was unable to accept the faith of the people in its entirety. His active mind infallibly performed its critical functions. Yet, up to a certain point, he obstinately persisted in submitting to the Orthodox discipline. He practiced the church rituals, he silenced his mind, and he forced himself into the expressions of faith on which the working people about him existed.

On a visit to Petersburg during Lent, he stopped in to see the family of his cousin at court. The entire family was Orthodox, but because of the Countess's age and poor health, they did not keep fasts. Tolstoy was indignant. He frowned all through dinner and was quite obviously annoyed. As soon as they rose from the table, he walked up to Countess Alexandra Tolstoy and asked her why they were not fasting. She explained and added, "You think it is wrong?"

"Certainly! If a man belongs to a church, the least he can do is obey its rules."

Tolstoy kept the fasts with unusual strictness. On one occasion he was ill and the doctor demanded that he break his fast. Tolstoy was afraid to follow his advice without permission from the church. He went to a monastery and asked the abbot for a dispensation.

In 1877 a teacher named Alekseyev appeared in Yasnaya Polyana. He was an avowed atheist and radical. He became very friendly with Tolstoy and at times took the liberty to express his surprise that Tolstoy, with his fine mind, his understanding, and his sincerity, should take the church rituals so seriously. On a clear, frosty day they were discussing the subject in the drawing room. Tolstoy was sitting in front of a window and watching the rays of the setting sun shining through the delicate patterns that the frost had made on the windowpane.

He said, "Look at these beautiful patterns, illuminated by the sun. We can see only the reflection of the sun in them, but we know that somewhere beyond the patterns is the real sun, which is the source of light and which creates the illusion we see. The people see only the images in religion, but I look further and see, or at least know, that there is a true source of light. This difference in our conception does not prevent us from worshiping together. We all see the reflection of the sun, and only the depth to which our gaze penetrates varies according to the state of our minds."

But regardless of what he said, at times Tolstoy became depressed. He simply could not become one with the working people around him.

Once when he came home from church, he said, "No, I cannot; it is too difficult! Standing among them, I can hear their fingers on their coats as they make the signs of the cross, and at the same time I can hear their suppressed voices as men and women whisper about the most trivial things in no way related to the church service. The men talk about their farms, and the women gossip, during the most solemn parts of the service, showing that they have not the least conception of what it means."

The difficulties went deeper. At first he had to believe in order to live. He tried to overlook the contradictions and the vagueness of the teachings, but gradually he was forced to admit that he could not understand two-thirds of the church services, and that the ingenious explanations could not help him. He had to be honest with himself about his faith.

The prayers for victory over the enemy and in praise of the Tsar embarrassed him. Before communion he could hardly force himself to proclaim his belief that, not bread and wine, but the flesh and blood of Christ were before him. He could not make himself believe it. He also found it difficult to participate in the celebration of holy days. With the exception of Christmas, most of them were commemorations of miracles, in which he had no faith. He could not understand or visualize the resurrection of Christ.

How often he envied the peasants for their lack of learning and their inability to reason! In the entire congregation his was the only unhappy mind that saw "the truth in the teachings of the church hopelessly interwoven with the thinnest threads of falsehood."

He suffered for three years.

Problems arose which had to be solved. He felt that these problems were solved by the church in a manner contrary to the very foundation of his faith. He could not sanction the animosity of the Orthodox church toward other denominations—Catholic or Protestant—and toward the sectarians. He thought, "If two assertions contradict one another flatly, neither can be the indisputable truth on which faith is based."

His soul could not make itself accept the attitude of the Orthodox church toward the war that was then being fought between Russia and Turkey, and toward capital punishment.

Tolstoy tried to find explanations that would satisfy him in the religious writers. He went to bishops and archbishops for advice. He visited monasteries and voiced his doubts to monks and hermits.

After watching the continuous stream of peasants on the high road as they passed Yasnaya Polyana on their way to Kiev to worship the relics of the saints, he finally decided to go there and to learn at first hand what the monks and abbots of the famous Kiev monastery were teaching the people.

But to no avail. No one could still the doubts that assailed him. On several occasions he became involved in arguments with the clergy and had to point out to them their lack of knowledge of the Holy Writ. Because of his passionate temperament, it frequently happened that a spirited argument only exhilarated him instead of setting his soul at rest. He felt that the more he listened to the clergy, the further he was from the truth and the nearer to perdition.

He was convinced that there was truth in the teachings. But unquestionably they were mixed with falsehood, and he had to find a way to separate the one from the other.

Once he was present while a priest was teaching the catechism to his children. Suddenly he found the scene revolting. The quick-witted children obviously disbelieved every word and could not conceal their contempt. Tolstoy felt a desire to express his faith in the form of a catechism. He tried it, but the task was extremely difficult.

4

At the beginning of Tolstoy's spiritual crisis the Countess was past thirty. When she was still a young girl, almost a child, she had already noticed the "changeable opinions" of her future husband. After she married him, this trait in the man she loved had no adverse effect on her. But a natural evolution gradually took place. Living in close relationship with the great man, she developed spiritually. As long as their tastes and interests coincided, she yearned with her entire being for the goal he had set for himself. She devoted her tireless energy to the care of the growing family and to helping her husband attain wealth and fame. Tolstoy, and everyone who knew her, agreed that the outstanding traits of her character were simplicity, directness, and sincerity. Together with these qualities, she had a certain spiritual tactlessness, which had been obscured by the charm of her youth and beauty. Now that she had reached maturity, this tactlessness became more noticeable. Her self-assurance, which Tolstoy had noted during the first years of their married life, became more pronounced with the years. She began by participating in all of her husband's interests, but as her evolution progressed, she turned away from some of his fads, such as physical labor on the farm, or work with the peasant children in the school. She became excited when Tolstoy's fads took him away from his literary work. She loved his creative genius, and besides, it meant money and fame, and the Countess had never been adverse to these. She was jealous of her husband's fads and no longer tried to hide her animosity. She frankly "despised" all the A-B-C's, arithmetics, grammars, and even schools, which took time from his "real work."

Inner religious upheavals were entirely foreign to her nature. With calm self-assurance, she considered herself a good Christian. Within the limits of social usage she responded to the demands of the church and brought up her children in a conventional Orthodox atmosphere.

Tolstoy's spiritual crisis was beyond her comprehension. Deaths and sicknesses upset her because they disrupted the carefree days of happiness which had preceded them. The vision of death which had so forcibly taken possession of her husband's imagination had no effect on her practical mind and common sense.

At first she thought it was merely a new fad. She was angry when he used God's name on all occasions and when he ended his letters to her with "God's will be done!" or "God have mercy on us!"

Later, as she watched him suffer, she decided that he was ill, and she insisted that he take proper steps to cure himself. She sent him for a rest cure and even went with the entire family to the Samara steppes, though she had no affection for their new home.

Sensing his spiritual agony, she tried to adjust herself. At least the new religious aberration that had taken hold of him was not a threat to the foundation of their family life, or a violation of the Orthodox conventions. She would have liked to tame her husband's excessive religious enthusiasm, but the twelve years she had lived with him had taught her that she could not influence his inward processes. They had to take their natural course. They had to be left to the healing influence of time.

The relations between them remained unchanged. Their love and their happiness never wavered.

During the most critical years of his spiritual struggle Tolstoy's letters to his wife were filled with tenderness, as of old. In 1876 he wrote her, "Sometimes I write to you without mentioning how I feel about you, because at the moment I would rather not, but during this separation I think tenderly of you every minute, and I want to fill my entire letter with endearments; good-by, my dear, my darling! I am so grateful for the feeling that I have for you and for knowing that you really exist."

In 1877: "Good-by, darling! I have not yet received a letter from you. When I am away from you, I try not to think about you. Yesterday I approached your desk, hurt myself by thinking about you, and immediately walked away so I would not miss you. At night I avoid looking in your direction."

In 1878: "If only God would grant that everything will be well during this separation! I relish this special, exalted, spiritual love for you which I feel when we are apart. The most important question now is should you, or should you not come here, to Samara? I am against it, and here is the reason: I know that above all you want to see me, and I would rather return than stay here."

Suddenly Tolstoy showed signs of questioning Orthodox beliefs and of revolting against the church. This was a new blow to the Countess. She was incapable of following her husband through all the tribulations of his search for truth, and to her his behavior often seemed unreasonable and illogical.

She had introduced a strict observance of all Orthodox customs by the household. When she sensed that her husband was assailed by doubts, she became even more punctual in obeying the decrees of the Orthodox church. Everyone in the family had to observe the fasts. Special food was prepared for the two teachers—the French tutor and the agnostic, Alekseyev. Once they were served some unusually appetizing-looking meat cakes. The butler left the dish on the sideboard. Suddenly Tolstoy said, "Ilya, pass me the meat." His son passed the dish. Tolstoy, with obvious relish, ate a meat cake and never observed another fast from that time on.

The Countess was at a loss.

Toward the end of that period she wrote, "Lev is completely buried in his religion. He has a peculiar stare, he is silent most of the time, he is no longer interested in this world, and he cannot think about mundane matters. . . .

"Lev reads, reads, and reads, and writes very little. He is in the habit of exclaiming, 'Now I can see it clearer!' or, 'If God will help me, what I am writing now will be very important!' Lev is, what he calls, working. Unfortunately, he is writing some religious disquisition. He reads and thinks until his head hurts, and all this to show that the Church dissents from the teachings of the Bible. I doubt if there are ten people in Russia who will be interested in this. I only hope that he will soon be tired of all this and will get over it as he gets over an illness. No one in the world can prescribe a cure for him, mentally or in any other way, and he is powerless to help himself."

In the meantime Tolstoy recovered from his depression. He had undertaken a tremendous critical work in an entirely new field, and he was confident that his mind would find the fundamentals, learn the truth, and soar high once again.

On October 22, 1879, he wrote in his diary:

"In this world there are many heavy people without wings. They struggle without rising. Some of them are strong like Napoleon. They leave terrible imprints on people, they uproot humanity, but they belong only to the earth. Other people, like the monks, gradually grow wings and slowly learn to rise and fly. Still other people are even lighter, have wings, and can rise easily when pushed and drop down again—the idealists are like that. Some of them have large, strong wings, but they drop among the others to satisfy their desires and break their wings— I am one of them. They flutter their broken wings, try to jump, and keep falling. When the wings are healed, I will soar again. God will help me. A few have divine wings. Out of love for humanity they descend to earth, fold their wings, and teach other people how to fly. When they are no longer needed, they fly away, like Christ."

Chapter Seven

HAD TOLSTOY undergone a complete spiritual transformation, and was there a definite spiritual crisis in his life?

Opinions differ. Tolstoy minutely described the torments of his spiritual rebirth in *Anna Karenina* and in his *Confession*. By taking into consideration various indications, the turning point can be traced to the late seventies. The year can be determined even more accurately. In 1884, when Tolstoy's thoughts had crystallized and when he had reached certain conclusions and a relative peace of mind, he wrote, "Five years ago I accepted the teachings of Christ and my life suddenly changed. I ceased to want the things I had wanted. What had seemed good appeared bad, and what had seemed bad appeared good. My experience was like that of a man who goes on an errand, halfway there decides that it is not necessary, and turns back. Everything that had been on his right is on his left, and what had been on his left is on his right. The desire to be as far as possible from home was transformed into a desire to stay at home. The direction in which my life was moving, and my very aspirations, changed. The good and the bad had changed places. This happened because I understood Christ's teachings, as I had not understood them until then."

This seems quite clear, but many students of Tolstoy, and even some people who were very close to him, have insisted that no violent change had taken place in him, and that everything he expressed in his later philosophical and religious writings had always been present in him. Among the evidence used to support this surprising theory is the entry in Tolstoy's diary dated March 5, 1855, in which, at twenty-six, he expressed a desire to create a new religion that would answer the spirit of the times. This entry is remarkable only because it was prophetic. But this isolated statement is not sufficient in itself. During Tolstoy's life he had many strange thoughts and dreams, and they were as significant as the prophetic dream of the heroine in *Anna Karenina*. Such sudden "prophecies" had no effect on Tolstoy's immediate and subsequent actions. Other forces guided Tolstoy. No one can say whether they were expressions of a subconscious urge, or whether they were merely coincidences linking passing thoughts with a remote future. The particular entry of March 5, 1855, was merely a dream of an ambitious young man. He wanted nothing less than to create a new religion for humanity. In the same way, three years earlier, he had dreamed of writing a "true, accurate history of present-day Europe," and believed this to be his "purpose in life." On another occasion he wrote in his diary, "I will devote the rest of my life to devising a plan of government based on the existing systems of elections, and forging a union between an elected aristocracy and the throne. This is sufficient for a productive life. Thank you, Lord, and give me strength!"

Such dreams incurred no obligations, and for twenty years after the entry he had made in 1855, even as late as the early seventies, Tolstoy had not given any serious thought to the creation of a new religion.

Nevertheless, the remarkable assertions made by the people who had been close to Tolstoy are partially true.

The elements of his subsequent writings and teachings can be found in Tolstoy long before the seventies. They are more frequent in his subconscious, intuitive, literary creations than in his diaries, articles, or letters. The seed was there. Like everyone else, young Tolstoy carried his potentialities within him, but in the seventies he underwent a violent crisis. Was it the only crisis in his life?

Tolstoy's outstanding characteristic was his changeability. Most people undergo a spiritual crisis, but Tolstoy's life was a succession of them.

In reading *War and Peace* the thought persists that both the heroes of the novel—Prince Andrew Bolkonsky and Pierre Besukhov—are spiritually close to the author. One represents what Tolstoy called "the mind of the mind" (reason, analysis, thought); the other, "the mind of the heart" (faith, synthesis, feeling). They are different, but because one is guided by reason and the other by his heart, they cannot be called opposites. They have one trait in common: their opinions, their convictions, and their conception of the world are constantly changing. Their convictions are likely to be reversed any moment. These changes are always a result of personal experiences: sickness, failure, surfeit, or the nearness of death. Suddenly a screw on which life depended snaps, their understanding of the interrelation of events falls apart, and chaos follows. Then, gradually, the destroyed world in their minds is rebuilt again, and this time seemingly on lasting foundations. Then other events occur, and everything falls apart again. Only the basic trait of their characters remains. No one can imagine the final stage of their spiritual development, or their final conception of the world. Death can stop these changes; but until death comes, their convictions, no matter how final, are subject to instant change. Their state is not one of continuous spiritual chaos, of continuous doubts and of continuous flux. At any given moment their convictions are strong and as firm as a rock. But tomorrow circumstances change, and the entire firm structure of a harmonious spiritual world is ruthlessly scrapped.

Such changes are less frequent in Prince Andrew and the process is more difficult. In Pierre Besukhov the constant change from religion to agnosticism is carried to the extreme and the fantastic phases of his spiritual development border on the ridiculous.

That quality which the philosopher Shestov described as the ability "to destroy and to recreate worlds" is dominant in Constantine Levin, the hero of *Anna Karenina.*

Tolstoy's life was filled with such crucial experiences. His character remained the same while the material for a change was accumulating. This material was reflected in his thoughts and in his literary work. Gradually it acquired a firmer and more conscious form. Then the break came. Sometimes the break was violent, as it was in the seventies; sometimes the change was milder and more gradual.

Almost all the elements of Tolstoy's future teachings can be found in his literary creations prior to 1879. But they were merely passing thoughts and experiences, and were not systematized into a philosophy. Nothing was emphasized. They were like the first glimmerings of light before the dawn. He laboriously studied the deceptive silhouettes of the objects that surrounded him, until the sun appeared and brilliantly illuminated everything. He believed he had arrived at a permanent "understanding." Unfortunately, he still had before him long days of prosaic reality filled with shadows, with new events, with new moods, and with new thoughts.

2

Tolstoy reached a stage when he felt that he must undertake a critical scrutiny of the teachings of the church. The results of his labors he presented in his *Critique of Dogmatic Theology.* He valued this work highly. Actually, its contents and its form leave much to be desired. With occasional references to the outward symbols of faith, the epistles of the Eastern Patriarchs, and the catechism, he took a textbook on dogmatic theology written by a bishop of the Russian Orthodox church and criticized it paragraph by paragraph. His book is full of violent attacks, sarcasm, and malice. He accused the church—"a gathering of idle, dishonest, ignorant people"—of subservience to the civil authorities and of a "conscious deception that serves as a means for one part of the people to govern the other." Thinking, educated men no longer paid any attention to the church. The people? Tolstoy felt that even the people were entirely indifferent to the church.

He attempted to prove that the church, with its "impenetrable forest of stupidity," is an anti-Christian organization. Church is superfluous. Christ never urged people to teach. He urged them to perform good deeds, so that others could see the reality of goodness and would glory in God. Faith consists, and always has consisted, of good deeds.⸻

An attempt was made to publish his *Confession* in one of the magazines, but the publication of the issue containing it was stopped and Tolstoy's article was banned by the censors. To publish the *Critique of Dogmatic Theology* was out of the question. Between Tolstoy and the government a fight ensued which increased his popularity tremendously. Illegally printed copies of his forbidden writings were sold in large quantities. At that time the Russian intellectuals were not much interested in religious questions, but the government's persecutions lent Tolstoy's thoughts a novel zest. In various parts of the country organizations were created for the avowed purpose of copying and distributing his religious writings.

Tolstoy now questioned everything. He felt that he must explore the original sources. He took the Greek texts of the Four Gospels, a number of important commentaries, and the best translations into modern languages. Using his recently acquired knowledge of Greek, he translated the Gospels word for word. Often, in lengthy annotations or even in full-length articles, he disagreed with the generally accepted interpretations and suggested new meanings. He painstakingly explained every deviation from the conventional translation, every added annotation, and every elimination, by comparing the various texts of the Gospels, by context, and by philologic reasoning. The deeper he delved into the subject, the more delighted and enthusiastic he became. Every step convinced him more firmly that Christianity was the strictest, purest, and fullest metaphysical and ethical teaching, unsurpassed before or since by human mind. At the same time, in trying to reconcile the Four Gospels, he reached a final conclusion that the teachings of the Christian churches had little in common with the original teachings of Christ, because they attempted the impossible: they tried to combine the philosophy of the Gospels with the Old Testament and with the more recent interpretations.

As the delighted and enthusiastic Tolstoy continued to make new discoveries, the tremendous work grew in size.

Twenty years later, in a foreword to a foreign edition of his *An Exposition of the Four Gospels,* the author considered his fanatical, "unforgettable" labor critically. In 1902 he wrote, "Unfortunately, I was carried away by zeal and enthusiasm. I was not satisfied to emphasize the easily understandable passages in the Gospels, to set forth the original teachings, and to omit the passages that fail to conform with the chief and basic meaning and which neither support nor contradict it. Instead, I even attempted to find for these obscure passages an interpretation that confirmed the general meaning. These attempts involved me in artificial and probably erroneous philological explanations, which weakened, instead of strengthening, the general meaning."

His book *What Do I Believe?* was the crowning achievement of these labors of Tolstoy's. He had worked on it during the entire year of 1883. It is a brilliant exposition glowing with faith. The results of the painful process that had taken so many years are presented with true Tolstoyan passion.

What were these unshakable truths that Tolstoy had discovered?

He categorically refused to accept the teachings of the church and Christian mysticism. To him Christ was not a God, but a teacher of truth. The Gospel has no need for the prestige of divine origin. Its basic teachings are inscribed in every soul. They are subject only to the dictates of the individual conscience.

The mundane teachings endorsed by the church have created a senseless, unhappy life on earth. This life terminates in death. Christ's teachings point to a purpose in life which cannot be destroyed by death. This purpose is peace, love, and unity among people. No one individual has the right to expect eternal life, but whenever anyone devotes his life to the furthering of love on earth, his work becomes indestructible. And the individual, after his physical death, will merge with the love existing in the cosmos, that is, with God.

In this way a truly Christian life acquires a purpose, despite the unavoidable death of the individual.

Growth of love on earth requires the elimination of temptations, which beset every man. The strength of temptations lies in the false promise of greater happiness in animal life. The Sermon on the Mount—the key to the understanding of the Gospels—gives five clear and precise commandments for fighting temptations. Tolstoy summarized them: (1) Do not be angry, (2) do not commit adultery, (3) do not swear, (4) do not resist evil with force, and (5) do not war—love the enemies of your people.

The observance of these five commandments eliminates everything evil from the life of the people. If the people observe them, the Kingdom of God will be on earth. This will give purpose to human lives despite the inevitability of individual death, and will make life blissful because every human heart thirsts for peace on earth.

The struggle against temptation requires a decided change in the way of living and in the social position of those in power.

"To be poor, to be a pauper, to be a beggar—that's what Christ taught. Without that no one can enter the Kingdom of God, without that no one can be happy on earth."

A transformation into a pauper or a beggar brings a man closer to nature and makes him free to do the work he loves—especially physical work. It makes it possible for him to be close to his family and it means free and loving communion with the rest of humanity, health, and a painless death.

People who persistently cling to worldly possessions are much more unfortunate than the last pauper.

"But no one will feed us and we will die of hunger," they answer, forgetting the words of Christ, "All these things shall be added unto you."

"Work without an ulterior motive and without the desire to accumulate wealth. Those who need your work will support your life and provide for your family."

Observance of this teaching is not difficult and does not involve suffering and privations. At the same time, it saves us from most of the sorrow which befalls us because of our worldly attitudes.

The twelfth and last chapter of the book is filled with grandiose enthusiasm. Tolstoy wrote:

"I believe that my own well-being on earth will become possible only when all people accept the teachings of Christ. I believe that these teachings can be observed easily and happily. I believe that even when these teachings are not observed by all and I alone among all people observe them, I still have no other way of saving my life from eternal perdition. I believe that, as long as I lived in accordance with the teachings of the world, I was miserable, and that only living in accordance with the teachings of Christ can give me happiness, which was intended for me by the Father of Life. . . . Everything that had seemed desirable and good: honors, fame, education, wealth, complexity and refinement in life, furnishings, food, clothes, and entertainment—all this appeared trivial and vulgar. Primitiveness, obscurity, want, coarseness, simplicity in furnishings, food, clothes, and entertainment—all this became for me essential and good. . . . I believe that I was given my sensible life—my light—so it would shine forth with deeds and not with words before other people, and make them praise the Father. . . . I believe that the only purpose of my life is to tend the light that shines within me and not to conceal it, but to hold it high so that other people can see it. . . . Because truth is imparted to other people only through deeds of truth."

These, briefly, were his new teachings. After reading this short summary, or even after reading Tolstoy's own eloquent book, they seem not very impressive. It is hard to believe that it would be simple and easy to follow these teachings in life. Tolstoy found his faith among the peasants. That any of them should have shared the convictions of the author of *What Do I Believe?* is extremely doubtful. A peasant is not easily persuaded that his position is enviable compared with the position of the nobles, the educated, and the rich. Besides, the faith of the peasant and the rules governing his conduct were based on the belief in individual eternal life and in reward and punishment "in the other world." Individual existence after death was contrary to Tolstoy's new faith.

No matter what others thought of him, Tolstoy was filled with the "delight of the knowledge of true life" and with the "desire and hope of realizing it at once." The first step in that direction was a complete change in the teacher's mode of life, "because truth is imparted to other people only through deeds of truth."

3

Tolstoy had neither the power nor the desire to hold back his discoveries and his "happiness." One of his first attempts to win a convert to his new faith was made in Petersburg. His true friend, his kindhearted cousin at court, had always longed to see him find a full and clear faith. Certain of success, he unexpectedly appeared at her apartment in the palace. Hardly taking time to greet her after a long separation, he began to tell her everything that had accumulated in his soul.

She remained silent.

"I see that you are carried away by my idea," he exclaimed at last.

"You are mistaken, my dear; I cannot even understand it."

He jumped from his chair as if something had stung him.

"How can you fail to understand it? It is so clear, and it can be explained in a few words. A window has been opened in my soul and through that window I can see God. Beyond that I need nothing. Not another thing!"

"What do you mean: not another thing? I realize that the most important thing is to believe in God, but before agreeing with you I must know how you believe in Him."

In reply, he eagerly began to prove the uselessness of the church and the harm that it had caused. He denied the divinity of Christ and the possibility of salvation through redemption.

Alexandra Tolstoy was strictly orthodox in her beliefs and

with her usual warmth defended the church he was abusing. A battle ensued, which lasted the entire day. Next morning she received a note, "Don't be angry with me for leaving without saying good-by. I simply could not. I am too much upset by the argument that took place yesterday. . . ."

He went away, and from then on serious differences arose between them. She wrote long and impassioned letters, considering that it was her sacred duty to persuade him to return to the fold of the Orthodox church. These letters irritated him. He demanded that she stop her attempts to "convert" him, "or, to express it politely, stop saying disagreeable things" to him. They had reached a break in their long friendship. At intervals they saw each other and exchanged letters, but their intimacy, already strained by his marriage, dwindled, became uncertain, and was never renewed.

His teachings had an even cooler reception within his immediate family. Here the question was not one of Orthodox faith. No one sympathized with or believed in his ideal of poverty. No one believed that people existed who would undertake to care for his large family in return for the physical labor performed by the aging Tolstoy. No one believed that he was able to do such work. No one could find any reason, or felt any desire, to change from the pleasant way of life that had been conceived and planned for them all by Tolstoy. He tried to relinquish his copyrights and to distribute his property among the poor. In vain—his efforts in this direction were met by determined resistance. He was told that if he were to attempt to distribute his property, the courts would appoint a guardian to manage his affairs, on the grounds of extravagance due to mental derangement. He was threatened with a commitment to an insane asylum.

These threats would probably never have been carried out, but they were made. Tolstoy's biographer, P. I. Biryukov, is very emphatic on the point. The manuscript of his book was read by Countess Tolstoy. She gave elaborate explanations, and made numerous annotations, but in regard to this particular incident annotations are conspicuously absent. Her brother, Stephen Behrs, mentioned the possibility of a state guardian in his reminiscences, which the Countess also read before they were published. The threats were undoubtedly made, but very likely they were made in the heat of a religious argument, which frequently flared up.

Tolstoy was emphatic, harsh, and irritable. Later he said, "I cannot blame Sonya. She cannot be blamed for not accepting my teachings. The things that she now clings to so persistently are the very things that for years I encouraged her to accept. Besides, during the early stage of my awakening I was too irritable and too insistent in my efforts to persuade her that I was right. At that time I presented my new understanding of life in such an unpleasant and unacceptable form that she felt a natural revulsion. Now I feel that she will never be able to attain the truth in the way that I have. The fault for closing the door to her is mine."

Tolstoy's teachings, when he presented them to his children, also met with little response. The eldest son, a good-natured young man, devoted to his father, was about to enter a university and took a definite stand against this new philosophy. He insisted that the existence of God could not be proved, that he had no way of judging whether the conclusions reached by his father were sound, that he felt no need for this philosophy, and that he enjoyed a physical life and believed in it. To the others, Tolstoy became a bore. They saw that he had grown solemn and irritable, that he quarreled with the Countess over trifles, and that he had changed from a gay and cheerful human being into a zealous reformer and fanatic.

His second son exclaimed, "How is it possible to reconcile the 'godly' life—the life of the beggar and peasant which appeals so much to Papa—with the unalterable, fundamental beliefs that have been instilled in us from our childhood: the unquestionable duty of having to eat soup and meat at dinner, to speak English and French, to prepare for school and the university, and to memorize our parts for amateur theatricals? We children often felt that we had not failed to understand Papa, but, on the contrary, he could no longer understand us because he was preoccupied with something all his own. . . . The old foundations of family life remained unshaken and just as selfishly necessary to every member of the family."

Among his friends his teachings fared no better. Fet visited Yasnaya Polyana in May, 1881. Tolstoy wrote in his diary, "A conversation with Fet and my wife. Christian teachings cannot be practiced. Are they useless? No, but they cannot be practiced. Have you ever tried to practice them? No, but they cannot be practiced."

Strakhov, the philosopher, visited Yasnaya Polyana, and Tolstoy, after several conversations with his devoted friend, saw him off with the harsh words, "He who is not with me is against me!" Strakhov wrote to him, "I felt as if you were reading me out of the church! What could I do?! The reason I defend my opinions is because I cannot do otherwise, and because I cannot see any virtue in self-deception. Whether you turn me away or not, I will remain true to you."

Necessity forced Tolstoy to survey and weigh his "discoveries." The only logical conclusion of his understanding of the teachings of Christ was a complete denial of the right of private property or of the possibility of acquiring private property in the future. The new life demanded that he forsake his family—"a man's enemies are those who are dear to him." He must leave, leave alone, disappear, cease being Tolstoy, be lost among the crowds, and become a nameless wanderer. He was not prepared to take this step. He knew that his wife and children loved him. He had lived with them so long that he suffered attacks of cruel, deadly loneliness during even a brief separation. In his new teachings he had asserted that a large and healthy family is one of the essentials of happiness. Later, when he had reached a very advanced age, in answer to a questioner who asked how he interpreted Christ's command to forsake the family, he said, "My understanding is that you should forsake worrying about them, as if they belonged to you. If the word 'forsake' is taken literally as meaning to leave them to their fate, it would contradict the very essentials of love, which is the ultimate purpose." But during the eighties even this calm and broad interpretation was foreign to him. He loved his family, he held that the family ties could never be severed, and that his duty was to look after them. He could not leave them. He could not force them to follow his teachings. Some compromise had to be found.

In the summer of 1881 he fell ill and once again had to go to take a rest cure in the Samara steppes. While there, he tried to arrange his business affairs, which were in a bad state. He suffered from the thought that he had left all the worries about the family and its affairs to his wife. She was in the last months of a pregnancy and had to make preparations to move the family to Moscow in the autumn. This move had been decided on some time before. The eldest son was about to enter a university. His daughter Tatyana had to be presented to society. With his new ideas, Tolstoy found it difficult to contemplate breaking up their country life and moving to the city, which he considered unhealthy. Evidently this caused numerous arguments, but after he had been in Samara and away from the family he began "to look forward to life in Moscow," and even to "believe in it." Around him he saw people who had settled on the land and who lived by the labor of their hands. What were they like?

"Nothing can more clearly prove the impossibility of living in accordance with one's ideals. . . . They are splendid people who, with all their hearts, with all their energies, strive for good and honest lives, but their lives and their families take different courses and the result is mediocrity. As an outsider, I can see that their mediocrity is good, but it is very far from the final purpose. Others apply the same measure to themselves and learn to be satisfied with it. Mediocrity in rationalization, mediocrity in national life, mediocrity everywhere . . ."

In almost every letter to his wife he confessed that he had been of little assistance in her many worries, and promised that when he returned he would be "good" in her sense of the word. He wrote, "I still think and feel the same way, but I have cured myself of the fallacious idea that other people must see things as I see them. I have wronged you greatly, my dear. I have wronged you unconsciously and unwittingly, and perhaps that absolves me. My only excuse is that, in order to work under high tension as I have, and in order to accomplish something, I had to forget everything. I confess that I have forgotten you too often. In the name of God and of our love, take care of yourself! Postpone everything until my arrival. I will do anything gladly and will do it well because I will try."

He even tried to find an idealistic basis for the compromise. "Family is a man's flesh," he wrote in his diary. "Leaving the family is another form of self-destruction. The family is a man's body, and he should not succumb to the temptation of serving the family instead of serving God. It is only an indicator of the place that the man should occupy in the economic scale. The family is flesh: as a weak stomach needs light food, so a spoiled family needs more than one accustomed to privations."

In 1882 he was looking for a place to live and bought a house in Moscow. During the next twenty-eight years this famous house in Khamovnichesky Lane was to see an endless procession of people of every class and nationality. The first winter in Moscow the Tolstoys spent in an apartment. The Countess insisted that the house had been bought contrary to her wishes. Whether this was so or not, it was Tolstoy who, in the autumn of 1882, was in Moscow supervising the repairing and remodeling of the house; it was Tolstoy who bought furniture, a brougham, a victoria, and two sleighs, and who gave orders to bring horses from Yasnaya Polyana. He attended personally to all the formalities in connection with his son's admission to the university and he took his eldest daughter to her first ball.

Reasons can be found for his every action, but he was living contrary to his own teachings. Somewhat later he wrote, "The excuses parents give for this mode of life are truly remarkable. 'I need nothing for myself,' says the parent. 'Life like this is a burden to me; but loving my children, I lead it for their sakes. In other words, I know from my own experience that our life is unhappy and, therefore, I bring up my children so that they will be unhappy too. To achieve this, I, out of my love for them, bring them to the city, which is filled with moral and physical plagues, surrender them into the hands of absolute strangers, who have only an ulterior interest in their education, and do my utmost to spoil my children physically, morally and mentally.' This reasoning is intended to justify the parents' senseless lives."

Conveniently as Tolstoy's accommodating mind explained things away, these thoughts tortured him. The good intentions that had filled the letters he wrote from Samara during the July of 1881 were never realized. After his return practically all the worries incident to moving the family to Moscow fell on the Countess. Tolstoy was ill. He was weak, depressed, and in a state of hopeless apathy. He could not sleep or eat, and he often sobbed like a child. During the first two weeks after they had moved to Moscow, his wife, watching him suffer, also cried every day.

In his diary for October 5, 1881, he wrote, "A month has passed—the most painful month of my life. We have moved to Moscow. Everyone is settled. When will they begin to live? Here things are done not because life demands them but because other people do them. What miserable people! There is no real life, only stench, stones, excesses, poverty, and vice. Having robbed the people and hired soldiers and judges to protect their orgies, the villains have gathered here and are celebrating. The plain people have no choice except to try to recover what has been stolen from them by catering to the passions of the robbers. The men are more ingenious. The women stay home, but the men polish floors, wash bodies in the public baths, and work as coachmen."

The Countess had a dream that she liked to describe. She dreamed that she was standing in front of a large church that was under construction. Before its doors towered a tremendous cross, on which was crucified the living Christ. Suddenly the cross began to move and, having circled the church three times, stopped before her. The Saviour looked at her, raised his hand,

and pointed at the golden cross that shone on the cupola above the church.

Actually, Tolstoy's attitude toward the Orthodox church disturbed the Countess least of all. Her happy days were over, and it was her fate to bear a heavy cross for the rest of her life. She worried chiefly about the future of the family and about the traditions of long years' standing in which her children had grown up and been educated. In 1914, in her autobiography, she wrote, "I was wondering how I could live, as long as my husband held such views; I was afraid, worried, and upset. With nine children, I could not turn like a weathercock and face in the direction in which my husband, with his constantly changing ideas, was going. His search for truth was warm and sincere, but in me it would have been stupid imitation, which would have been unhealthy for the family. . . . If, in accordance with my husband's wishes, all of our property had been given away to anyone who came along, I should have been left without a thing and with nine children on my hands. I should have had to work in order to feed them, to sew and wash, and to let them grow up without any education. My husband, true to his calling and talent, could not have done anything except write."

While the family arguments were still taking place, the Countess held the same views, but she expressed them more vehemently and brusquely. In answer to his plans for a change in the management of the farm and to his complaints about the general poverty that surrounded him in Samara during the summer of 1881, she wrote, "The farm can continue as it has. I am opposed to any change. If there are losses it will not be the first time; if there are profits and the money is given away, my children and I will not benefit by it. You already know my views about helping the poor. You cannot feed thousands of people in Samara or anywhere else, but if you see a needy case, and know that a certain family lacks food, a horse, a cow, shelter, or any other necessity, you must help at once. You should give because you pity them and because it is right."

Next year when he was in the country again, she wrote, "As

soon as I awoke, I was sad and depressed because of your letter. Things are going from bad to worse. I begin to believe that if suddenly a happy man can see only the horrible things in life and can shut his eyes to everything good, something must be wrong with his health. You should try to cure yourself. I say this because it seems so obvious, and without any ulterior motive. I am awfully sorry for you and if, without becoming irritated, you would think about my words and about your condition, perhaps you would find the answer. Your mental depression has been apparent for some time. Once you said, 'I wanted to hang myself because I had no faith.' What has happened now? Why are you unhappy now that you have a faith? Are you only now realizing that the world is full of hungry, miserable, and mean people? Look around you more carefully: you will find some gay and healthy people, some happy and kind people. I hope God will guide you, because I am helpless."

Early in 1883 she wrote, "Lev is calm, he works, he writes articles, but occasionally he becomes violent about city life and the extravagant mode of living. He hurts me, though I know that he cannot help himself. He is a leader, he goes ahead of the crowd and points the way that others must take. I belong with the crowd. I move with the crowd, with the crowd I see the light of a lantern carried by any leader, including Lev, and I recognize it as a light. But I cannot move any faster: my crowd, my surroundings, my habits hold me back."

On June 27, 1883, in a letter to her husband, she wrote, "I am still reading your article, or, better still, your creation. Obviously nothing can be said against the assertion that it is good to be perfect, and that it is necessary to remind people constantly that they should be perfect, and to point out to them the ways in which they can reach perfection. But I must confess I find it difficult to put aside all the playthings in life with which I am accustomed to play. Everyone—and I especially so—persistently clings to playthings and enjoys it when they sparkle, make a noise, and amuse. Without discarding them, we cannot be perfect and cannot be Christians. And we will not give away our clothes, we will not love only one 'wife' in our lives, and we will not throw down our weapons, because we should be locked up if we were to try."

The reasoning in these letters is sound, sincere, and unassuming. According to Tolstoy, sincerity is the most valuable quality in a person. There was a reason why, in *Anna Karenina,* he was so touched by the sincerity and truthfulness of Kitty Shcherbatsky.

Unfortunately, in their daily lives they showed much less restraint about their differences. They were impatient, passionate, emphatic people. When in 1882, Tolstoy decided to study Hebrew, the Countess, who had eagerly waited for his return to creative writing, became extremely irritated because he was "wasting strength on trifles." She neither wished nor was able to conceal her disappointment. They quarreled almost daily over his violent views, over his depressed moods, and especially over the slightest material losses that threatened the family. His diaries during this period reflect a state of hopeless misery. In 1884 he wrote, "I find it very difficult to be with the family. I find it difficult because I cannot share their feelings. All their joys, examinations, social successes, music, clothes, shopping—all this I consider misfortune and an evil, but I cannot explain this to them. I try to talk to them, but they seem unable to grasp my words. They refuse to think about the meaning of my words, and instead feel that I am inconsiderate to mention the subject. In my weaker moments—and this is one of them—their heartlessness amazes me. How can they fail to see that during the last three years I have not only suffered, but that I have been deprived of my life? I have been assigned the role of a grumbling old man, and I am nothing else in their eyes. If I should share their lives, I should be disloyal to the truth, and they would be the very first to point out my inconsistency to me. If I continue sadly to watch their insane behavior, I am a grumbling old man like all other old men."

He felt that he was being "swamped" in their life. At times he was overcome by a sense of "mortal frailness," at others his emotions ran away and he rebelled. He believed that his wife's lack of self-restraint and irritability were the cause of every-. thing. He had a feeling that "a stalking tiger" was near him. He wrote, "I can stand stupidity and dullness of soul, but not when they are accompanied by impudence and self-assurance." He persuaded himself that everything could have been adjusted in the family if he had not lacked a "loved and loving wife." He began to think about going away. "Actually, of what use to them am I? What good will my sufferings accomplish? No matter how great the hardships of a tramp's life are—and they are not so great!—they cannot under any circumstances compare with this heartache! . . . If only I could be sure of myself, because I certainly cannot go on with this insane life. Even they would derive some good from it. If they still have any semblance of a heart, they would be forced to think."

Describing his wife's constant "explosions" and outbreaks of "malice," he admitted that at times he was unable to control his temper.

"She came to me and plunged into a hysterical scene. She said that nothing would change, that she was miserable, and that she would leave me. I felt sorry for her, but I also realized that the situation was hopeless. . . . As long as I live, she will be a stone tied with a rope around my neck and around the necks of the children. . . . Probably I should learn not to sink even when I am dragging a stone, but what about the children? Probably they should learn too. I am sorry that I am so blind. I tried to calm her, as if she were a sick person."

At other times the Countess, unaware of the extent of the break between them, was serene and calm.

He could not endure these constant emotional changes. One evening in June, 1884, he was mowing the grass in the garden. After a swim he returned, gay and cheerful, to the house. The Countess, who expected to give birth to a child any day, was unusually nervous. She met her husband with heated recriminations about his intention of selling the horses, saying that he wanted to get rid of them merely because he had no use for them himself. Suddenly he was overwhelmed by an unbearable weight. He broke off the stormy argument, went to his room, gathered a few things, and with a sack on his back left the house, saying that he intended never to return. The excitement brought on labor pains, and her physical and mental suffering seemed unbearable. She prayed God to let her die, while he, all alone, was walking down the Tula highway, leaving behind him the "house inhabited and managed by insane people."

But he remembered that she was about to give birth to a child and turned back. At home "bearded ruffians"—his sons—were playing whist. Other members of the family were on the croquet ground. He walked straight to his study and stretched out on the sofa, but he could not sleep. At three o'clock in the morning she came down to see him.

"Forgive me! The pains have begun and perhaps I shall die."

At seven in the morning their daughter Alexandra was born. Because of her mother's condition, the child had to have a wetnurse.

Thirty years later the Countess asserted, "I can never forget that horrible, ghastly June night!"

In 1884, before his emotions had subsided, he wrote in his diary, "If anyone guides our destinies, I want to shame him. Our life is too complicated and too cruel—too cruel to her. I can see that she is moving faster and faster toward perdition and horrible inward tortures."

Among the many outbreaks that occurred in their complex relationship the scene that took place in December, 1885, is especially remarkable. The Countess described it to her sister Tatyana:

"The same thing that has happened so often before has happened again. Lev worked himself into a state of fury and depression. I was writing at my desk when he came in. I looked around and his face terrified me. We had been getting along beautifully; not a single disagreeable word, not a single argument. 'I have come to tell you that I want a divorce; I cannot live like this. I am going to Paris or to America.' Please understand, Tatyana, that I could not have been more surprised if the house had collapsed on me. Dumfounded, I asked: 'What has happened?' 'Nothing, but if you keep adding to a load, a horse stops and cannot go any farther.' I had no notion of what he meant. Then he began to scream, to hurl accusations and harsh words at me, and the scene became more disgusting every minute. I tried to keep my temper but when he finally said that 'the very air around me was infected' I gave orders to bring my trunk and began to pack. I wanted to visit you for at least a few days. The children rushed in crying. Tatyana said: 'I am going with you. What is this all about?' He begged me to stay. I gave in, and then suddenly hysterical tears began. It was horrible! . . . Just imagine, Lev shaking all over and convulsed with sobs. I felt so sorry for him. Four of the children—Tatyana, Ilya, Helen, and Mary—were screaming at the top of their voices. I was stunned. I could not talk or cry. I kept wanting to say something foolish, but I was afraid to utter a word and was silent. I remained silent for three hours. I could not have said anything if my life had depended on it! That is the way it all ended. But the bitterness, the misery, the hurt, the sickly feeling of being a stranger, are still with me. I ask myself until I am almost insane: what have I done? I have not been out of the house for a minute, I have been working on the manuscripts until three in the morning. I have been calm. I love everyone. I have treasured these peaceful days more than any others and suddenly all this. Why?"

The last vestiges of their love for each other were about to be destroyed.

Chapter Eight

EARLY in 1882 a population census was to be taken in Moscow. Among other people prominent in public life, Tolstoy received an offer to supervise the work of the precinct workers. He accepted, and chose as his district a part of Moscow that was inhabited by the poor.

In preparation, he visited a public lodging house located in his district. In the December twilight a large crowd of scantily dressed people, shivering in the cold, had gathered for the doors to be opened. Tolstoy was aghast. After talking with them, he called a street vendor and offered the unfortunates some hot drinks. The vendor's samovar was emptied in a few minutes. Having distributed among them what little money he had with him, Tolstoy, surrounded by his new acquaintances, entered the gates, which had been opened at last. Stench, filth, and disease were everywhere.

Feeling like a criminal, he returned to his comfortable home and settled down to a five-course dinner, which was served by waiters in white gloves. The contrast was too much for his imagination. With sudden fury, he began to wave his hands wildly, and choking with tears, shouted at his family and guests, "It's impossible to live like this! . . . It's impossible to live like this! . . . It's impossible! . . ."

He regained his calm, but he decided to act. He wrote an impassioned article, the proofs of which he read to the city council. He appealed to the two thousand people working on the census to ascertain the needs of the people in the course of their work and, of their own accord, to maintain their contacts with the needy after their work was completed. He also urged them to do everything in their power to aid the unfortunates.

He called on some of his wealthy acquaintances and exacted promises of contributions.

His article was published and met a warm response, but the entire undertaking was a failure.

In his new confession, *What Are We to Do?*, Tolstoy explained the reasons.

He lacked the patience to collect the money that had been promised him, and the money, as he had feared, was of little use. In the spring, anxious to finish his charitable experiment and to return to Yasnaya Polyana, he was at a loss how to dispose of the thirty-seven rubles that remained in his possession.

In the slums of Moscow he found that working people not only earned their living but at times had to help others. Tolstoy came face to face with the dregs of society, consisting of the lowest type of prostitutes, of homeless children, and of people who for one reason or another had lost everything in life. Money alone could not help these people. Could they be helped by love, by friendly, brotherly interest, and by diligent, painstaking work? Though he was not aware of it, Tolstoy had no real sympathy for such people. Maxim Gorki, whom Tolstoy liked personally, tells in his reminiscences of the obvious displeasure Tolstoy showed while he was listening to the reading of *The Lower Depths* in the Crimea in 1902. He constantly interrupted the author, left the room several times, was barely able to control his disgust, and when the reading was finished asked Gorki angrily, "Why did you write this?"

In Moscow, in 1882, the unfortunates in the public lodging houses, though he tried to help them, aroused no feeling of love in Tolstoy. Strangely enough, his only reaction was anger, directed not against the objects of his philanthropy, but against the privileges for which they were striving. After seeing this devastating poverty, and not knowing how to help, Tolstoy determined to find its causes. "The truth" became "clear" to him only three years later.

This truth was: "Justice cannot prevail, as long as some people feast continuously while others fast and work." By devious means a few unscrupulous people have succeeded in cornering the magic, all-powerful rubles, and with that weapon have virtually conquered the rest of the people and have forced them to work. After robbing the peasant of his birthright, these privileged "gentlemen" have moved to the city, where they lead "insanely luxurious lives" that tempt and demoralize the poor, who are forced to follow the wealthy to the city so that they can beg the crumbs off their tables. How can need be satisfied with stolen money? What love, what fellow feeling, what friendship can exist between the rich and the poor? The rich will never be trusted. Brotherly and friendly relations, without which real help cannot be given, will never exist.

Tolstoy's new book, *What Are We to Do?*, was filled with striking pictures of social inequality. Forgetting that "those who work shall be fed," he wrote with stark, merciless realism about the poverty in the city and about the hopeless lives led by the working people in the city and in the country. By contrast he drew a picture of continuous feasting among the wealthy, the prominent, and well educated. Tolstoy had not overlooked himself or his family. He systematically studied the historical development of all privilege and especially the accumulation of wealth. He saw it as a "lien on the work of the poor," by the assistance of which serfdom had been established again. He argued that "we have no justification for our privileged position. We have usurped it through trickery, and we are holding it through lies." Money cannot provide relief. "I saw that any use of money, the purchase of any article, even the process of giving it away, is nothing but a form of presenting an obligation against the poor, or, at best, of passing it for presentation by someone else. The absurdity of what I was trying to do became clear to me—I was trying to help the poor by drawing on the poor.

"I stood up to my ears in mud and was trying to pull others out of it.

"Then what is the solution? What are we to do?

"As soon as I understood what constituted wealth, what constituted money, not only what I had to do, but what others had to do became clear and obvious to me. Actually, I merely realized what I had known for a long time—that truth which has been passed to the people since the ancient times by Buddha, by Isaiah, by Lao-tse, by Socrates, and particularly clearly and convincingly by Jesus Christ and by his predecessor, John the Baptist. In answer to the people's question, 'What are we to do?' John the Baptist gave a simple, forthright, and clear answer, 'He that hath two coats, let him impart to him that hath none; and he that hath meat, let him do likewise.' (Luke 3:10–11) The same thing, but even more clearly, was said by Christ."

What were the people like Tolstoy to do to carry out the simple, plain, and clear advice contained in the New Testament, if various considerations and circumstances stood in their way?

Apparently the answer to this question was also very "simple and clear." A person must repent sincerely and realize that "nonparticipation in the struggle for a livelihood is tantamount to destruction of other lives." A person must like simple things and scale down his habits and expectations to the level of a peasant. He must be able to provide heat, clothes, and shelter for himself, and, most important of all, to grow food with his own hands.

Tolstoy felt that food divided every man's day into four parts: before breakfast, from breakfast until dinner, from dinner until supper, and from supper until bedtime. Every man's activities can also be divided into four groups: muscular activity, the work of the hands, feet, shoulders, and back, and heavy labor that makes a man sweat; activity of the fingers and wrists, work demanding skill, artisanship; activity of the mind and of the imagination; social activities with other people. The products that every man consumes can also be divided into four classifications. Every man uses: first, products of heavy labor, such as bread, meat, buildings, wells, dams, and roads; second, products of artisanship, such as clothes, shoes, and utensils; third, products of mental activity, such as the sciences and arts; fourth, the fruits of social intercourse among people, such as friendship and community undertakings. A man would do well to arrange his day so that all four types of his abilities are exercised, and so that he will contribute all four types of the products that he consumes. In this way he can occupy each of the four stages of the day: first with physical labor, second with mental work, third with artisanship, and fourth with social activities.

What, then, is the final answer to the question: What are we to do?

Until the time comes when we can relinquish our rights to private property and to the possession of money—rights for which we depend on force—we are to exercise them as little as possible. We are to participate, through physical labor, in the production of the necessities of life. We are to make other people see the unfairness and inhumanity of unnatural rights, based on privileged social position, wealth, or education.

This was Tolstoy's personal solution of the world problem of the relation between wealth and poverty.

He insisted that by fulfilling this program he found it easier to live. The feeling that he was guilty, that he was committing a crime, had lessened. The desire for mental activities was stimulated by physical labor. The heavier the physical labor, the "stronger, more energetic, gayer, and kindlier" Tolstoy felt.

While this process of self-improvement was under way, and while the proper adjustments in life in accordance with the new program were being made, the inhabitants of the public lodging house were forgotten.

Two years earlier, with fiery zeal and remarkable eloquence, he had advocated a break with social privilege, and a life of poverty, wandering, anonymity, and physical labor sufficient to feed oneself and one's family. All this seemed easily and simply realized. All this had to be done in order to exemplify the Christian teachings through deeds.

This had failed, though not entirely through his fault. He had had to find compromises and to be satisfied with "a middle road." Now, as in his youth, the revolutionary change was replaced by the new "rules of life." Substitutes were found for poverty and for a peasant way of life. Simplifying his life, lowering his needs to a minimum, dividing his time between supplying his own needs and helping others—these were the new ideals.

This was a new phase of development. The actual significance of this way of life is unimportant. Anyone can see that to live in accordance with the rule of the four basic activities may be very healthy, but that it is feasible only for a man of independent means.

2

In October, 1888, Tolstoy summarized his new program of life in a letter: "To describe its practical application in a brief, inadequate, but basically correct way, is to say: a man must decrease his demands on other people's work as much as possible, and if necessary begin to work for other people. He must do so cleanly and lovingly, avoiding such vices as drunkenness and immorality, which hurt his body and soul. In doing this, he should try not to hurt the people close to him or the people who stand in his way."

As far back as 1881 Tolstoy had tried to take an active part in the physical labor of the peasants. During the winter in Moscow he made a habit of going to Vorobyov Mountains, a near-by suburb, where he worked with the woodcutters and discussed life with them. In the country he began to take part in the field work.

The Countess was not in the least annoyed by these "eccentricities." She considered physical labor good for her husband's health, and her only worry was that in his enthusiasm he would overtax his strength.

Later, when Tolstoy's new convictions formed a complete system, when he began making speeches against the "extravagant" style in which the family lived, and especially when these accusations—which at times were most harsh—ceased to be confined to the family circle, and appeared as articles in the press, the Countess took a definitely hostile stand toward the entire "Tolstoyan" movement. In moments of anger and irritation she even questioned her husband's sincerity. She believed that all this was nothing but a way of emotionalizing religion. Usually Tolstoy tried to guide the ship safely across the shoals of family scenes, but he persisted in his way of life. The Countess became accustomed to shutting her eyes to his behavior. Her problems in life were confined essentially to finding ways of protecting the family income, of protecting and even increasing her children's financial resources, of defending the traditional forms in their upbringing, and of insuring a social career for them. In these respects she was adamant.

In 1883 Tolstoy decided to rid himself of the management of his estate. Entering his wife's room he said excitedly, "I find it so difficult to own and manage property, that I have definitely decided to rid myself of it, and I am appealing to you, first. Take everything—the house, the land, the copyrights—and manage them in any way you can. I will give you a power of attorney."

"Why?"

"I consider property an evil and I want none of it."

"So you want to pass the evil on to me? To the person who is closest to you?"

The Countess cried, "I don't want it, and I will not take a thing."

Eventually she agreed and received from him a power of attorney enabling her to manage the property as she saw fit.

The Countess wrote: "Inexperienced, without any money, I became determined to learn the business of publishing books, and of selling and taking subscriptions for my husband's works. I also had to manage the country estate and all the other business. With a large family and with no experience, I found it extremely difficult. On many occasions I had to make trips to Petersburg to take up matters with the Government censors."

The Countess consulted many of her friends and Dostoyevsky's widow, who, even before her husband's death, had taken over the publishing of his works. Matters progressed wonderfully. After overcoming a certain amount of opposition on the part of the booksellers, the Countess succeeded in putting the sales of her husband's works on an exceptionally profitable basis. Beginning with 1886, she published the books herself. Before that, Tolstoy's complete works appeared only every five or six years. The Countess had her second edition (the sixth in the general count) ready in 1887. Toward the end of the same year a demand for a new edition became evident. The Countess's fourth edition (the eighth in the general count) appeared in 1889. Her management of the country estate was equally successful.

Her work with the family continued to expand. She wrote, "The father withdraws more and more from the life of the family." She had nine children to care for; and the older they grew, the more complicated were the problems of their education and of their relations with the family. The father drew further and further away from them, and finally refused altogether to take part in their education, giving as his excuse that they were taught in accordance with standard programs and with the catechism of the Orthodox church, which he considered as evil.

Tolstoy began simplifying his mode of life with clothing. He decided to dress like a peasant. In his personal life he refused the services of a servant, he swept and cleaned his own room, his clothes, and his shoes. Beginning with the stove in his own room, he later undertook to look after the stoves in the entire house. One winter he took over cutting and preparing kindling and logs. The water came next. Tolstoy rose while it was still dark, went to the well, pumped enough water for the household, and dragged a barrel of icy water to the kitchen on a sled. In 1884 he decided to learn shoemaking. A couple of low benches were installed in the small room next to his study, which became filled with a smell of leather. A cobbler whom he knew came to see Tolstoy and they spent hours together working on shoes. Soon Tolstoy persuaded his daughters to wear shoes of his make.

In the country he cut the grass in his extensive gardens and frequently joined the peasants in community mowing. The peasants around Yasnaya Polyana mowed the grass on shares, receiving half of the hay for their work. Tolstoy joined first one crew, then another, helping them, and leaving them the grass he had cut. Gradually he began to plow and harrow, frequently helping peasant families that were short-handed in working their own land. In certain instances he took on himself the entire cycle of farm labor on the land of some widow who lacked the money to pay a hired man. His family became accustomed to his strange behavior. His daughters—especially the second daughter, Mary—frequently gave him a hand. Occasionally the example set by the host was followed by his guests.

For some time the life of the privileged classes had been personified for Tolstoy by "His Highness, the Prince Blokhin." This was the name assumed by a feeble-minded peasant who wandered in the vicinity of Yasnaya Polyana. During the Turkish war he had been a grain buyer attached to an official in the quartermaster's department. His obsession was that he could live like a gentleman without work and receive what he needed from the powers that be. He called himself "His Highness, the Prince Blokhin, in charge of military supplies of all kinds." He claimed that he had "held all ranks" and, having retired, was to "receive from the Tsar an open bank account, clothes, uniforms, horses, conveyances, tea, peas, servants, and all other necessities." To the question, "Haven't you any desire to work?" Blokhin always answered, "Much obliged, the peasants will attend to that."

"But what if the peasants too have no desire to work?"

"Machines have been invented to lighten the work of the peasants. They will have no difficulties."

"What are you living for?"

"To pass the time away."

According to Tolstoy, all privileged classes suffered from the "Blokhin mania." His family was no exception. Actually, his children made an exceptionally good impression on outsiders. Most of them were charming boys and girls, straightforward, sincere, and kind. Their attachment for Tolstoy had not diminished in the least, but gay, young life was bubbling within them, and Tolstoy's senile theories could not control it. The young people neither wished nor intended to resign their social position

for the sake of a principle, but they willingly accepted a simpli-
fied mode of life and joined eagerly in the work. Tolstoy's example attracted them. They often went into the fields and noisily
took part in the peasants' labors. Entire crews, made up of themselves and their guests, competed with each other. Ilya even
learned to make shoes.

Once the Countess became infected with the "emotionalism,"
dressed in peasant clothes, and took part in turning hay. The
peasants around Yasnaya Polyana remembered how Tolstoy
brought a visiting Japanese newspaperman to help them with
their work. They watched with great interest while the old
painter Gay laid bricks for a stove in a hut that Tolstoy was
building for a poor widow.

Tolstoy had not undertaken physical labor "to pass the time
away." As always, he was sincere and serious.

The Yasnaya Polyana peasants sensed this. They were accustomed to the eccentricities of wealthy landowners, but they said
that Tolstoy worked "for his soul." But they could not have
been expected to understand the differences that existed between
Tolstoy and his wife, and to realize why the kind and wealthy
landowner refused to help the poor with his money. The average
peasant totally lacked the quality of idealizing labor, which the
great writer was so eager to find in them. The peasant was in
the habit of saying that "poverty and not choice was behind the
plow." He was unable to conceive the idea that the necessity to
work could be a factor in the life of the gentry. In reality, Tolstoy never had the opportunity to support his entire family by
his physical labor. He certainly could not deceive himself on this
score, and at times he complained that his "physical labor was
practically useless because it was not an absolute necessity."

At this point his theories and their application parted company. He had a remarkable trait in his character. Whenever he
considered reality critically, he saw real life, and he described
the hardships suffered by the working classes with remarkable
depth, truth, and force. But as soon as he left social criticism for
abstract thought, he immediately forgot reality and began to

build castles in the air. According to his theory, expressed in *What Do I Believe?*, everyone who toiled received a just reward and therefore a working man would always find ways to support his family.

Apparently fate decided to bring Tolstoy back to earth by a concrete example.

In the middle eighties, Isaac Feinerman, a pleasant young Jew, arrived in Yasnaya Polyana. He was carried away by Tolstoy's ideas and had decided to serve the Russian people. Feinerman came to the country to work as a teacher. According to the custom of the time, this was altogether out of the question for a Jew. He joined the Orthodox church, but the primary-school section of the Ministry of Education still refused to employ him as a public-school teacher. He decided to stay in Yasnaya Polyana and in accordance with the spirit of Tolstoy's gospel to assist those who needed his work. He lived in a peasant hut, ate peasant food, reduced his requirements to a minimum, and worked diligently. Soon after he arrived, he was joined by his wife, a beautiful young Jewess, and by his child. They were in desperate straits, and in order to obtain enough food for the child the woman was forced to beg. Tolstoy gave her some copying work, for which he paid her, but she could not endure the life and left her husband. Feinerman persisted in his work. One evening he came to see Tolstoy, who asked him to read something aloud. Suddenly, while he was reading, Feinerman turned pale, lost consciousness, and dropped to the floor. He had worked the whole day without eating and was exhausted by hunger.

This incident shook Tolstoy deeply. He was never able to forget it.

In the early eighties Tolstoy, surrounded by a large, gay, cheerful family, felt that he was lonesome. He unburdened his soul to a correspondent (personally unknown to him), in whose letters he detected sympathy for his ideas. He wrote that no one could conceive how lonesome he, Tolstoy, was and how his true "self" was despised by those around him.

In her old age the Countess still remembered that letter. In

1909 she said, "I stuck a copy of it in an envelope, across which I wrote, 'A letter to Engelhart, whom Lev has never known or seen.' Let others judge this as they see fit. I was very much hurt by that letter."

To satisfy his mind, Tolstoy sought out people who held similar ideas. In 1881 he heard about a peasant, Siutayev, who in his own way had reached the same conclusions as Tolstoy. Tolstoy decided to investigate him personally. He went to visit friends who owned land in the Province of Tver. Siutayev lived within nine miles of their home. Tolstoy found a friendly family and a charming old peasant who interpreted the Gospel in his own way. He read with difficulty, and could not write at all. Siutayev advocated a life based on love for one's fellow man and on denial of the right of private property. In 1877 one of Siutayev's sons, a conscientious objector, had refused to serve in the army and was serving a prison sentence. The old man was not poor, but of his own free will he performed the duties of the village shepherd—a task despised by everyone—because he wanted to be certain that the cattle were properly fed and watered. Siutayev decided to spread his teachings through the offices of the Emperor, Alexander III. He went to Petersburg to ask the Tsar "to issue orders for the good of the people to teach the Gospel in accordance with Siutayev's interpretations." Tolstoy and this naïve idealist became great friends. Seeing his new friend off to the station, Siutayev harnessed a horse, but as a matter of principle, refused to bring a whip. They traveled at a slow pace, and talked "heartily in a brotherly fashion" about the salvation of humanity. In the meantime the horse wandered into a ravine. The wagon turned over, and the two dreamers literally were brought down to earth. Later Siutayev often came to Moscow to visit Tolstoy, who took him to preach in some of the fashionable salons, where at one time he was quite the rage. He died in 1892, and his followers disappeared.

Tolstoy's growing desire for new, sympathetic friends was gradually satisfied.

The first one on the scene was the well-known painter Gay.

In 1882 he was living in his small country place in the Ukraine, where he happened to come across one of Tolstoy's articles. He was prepared for it by a long mental process that he had undergone. He immediately realized what he needed and at once became converted to the new faith. Impulsively, he rushed to Moscow, burst in on Tolstoy, embraced him, kissed him, and until his death remained his tender friend and respectful admirer. This fifty-year-old idealist, with large, naïve blue eyes and long gray locks, immediately became the favorite of the entire Tolstoy family. He painted a portrait of the Countess, and she enjoyed posing for him in a black velvet dress trimmed with Alençon lace. But when he finished, "Grandfather Gay" announced that the result was a portrait of "an aristocrat in a velvet dress with at least forty thousand rubles in her pocket." He was outraged by his own criticism and destroyed the canvas.

The appearance of Chertkov in the Tolstoy household had an entirely different character. This event took place toward the end of 1883 and had serious consequences for Tolstoy and for his entire family.

Chertkov was the son of a governor general. His mother had occupied a position at court. He had been educated with the Emperor Alexander III. The Chertkovs had, in the Province of Voronezh, a large country estate, which brought in a yearly income of forty thousand rubles. A handsome, brilliant officer in the most aristocratic regiment, the Horse Guards, Chertkov was a great social success. The ladies ran after him, he led a wild life, he dissipated and gambled. But there were times when brilliant social successes failed to satisfy him, and he became more and more frequently assailed by periods of doubt and religious yearning. Early in 1881 he persuaded his parents to give him their permission to resign from the army, and went to live in the country so that he could "find ways of approaching the peasants who were feeding them, and of working on their behalf." He led an extremely simple life, studied the question of self-government for the peasants, and worked hard to found a number of self-supporting institutions for the poor. He had been hearing about

Tolstoy for a long time and in 1883 came to see him. Their first meeting was the beginning of a friendship that lasted for many years. At last Tolstoy had found a real friend and follower. Not just any man, but a man obviously sincere, who had the strength of his convictions and who had sacrificed much for the sake of his new understanding of life. Chertkov impressed Tolstoy by his sincerity, his way of saying things without fear of consequences, his calm assurance, and his directness of manner. Later, many people expressed surprise at the tremendous influence Chertkov exercised over Tolstoy's genius, which was incomparably greater. But Chertkov's fanaticism, his purism in his neo-Christian faith, even his pedantry filled the blank spots in Tolstoy's broad and easily changeable nature. Acquaintances who had no reason to be prejudiced against Chertkov felt that he was not altogether normal.

Professor Lazursky, who during his youth had been a teacher in the Tolstoy household, wrote in his reminiscences, "I found it difficult to understand that man, and I never could fathom him. At times I felt that eyes like his could exist only in an icon, at others I felt that Chertkov had something unhealthy about him, that he had more than the usual limitations."

Chertkov was not easy to get along with, probably because of his harsh way of saying things, though when he wanted to be polite he always charmed people. In his determination, he often appeared naïve, and found himself in decidedly awkward situations.

This "friend" became the apostle of the "Tolstoyan" movement.

In general, Tolstoy's teachings had gradually spread and were attracting people of every description in increasing numbers. Drawn by his outspoken anarchistic opinions, revolutionaries and even terrorists frequently came to see him. These people usually came secretly, were disappointed by their conversations with Tolstoy, and vanished forever. They were known in the Tolstoy family as the "dark ones." Later the family applied the same nickname to all the Tolstoy followers who sought friendship with the great writer. Slowly a world apart formed around Tolstoy—a world that his family viewed with serious misgivings. But at the same time, Tolstoy's solitude in his ideals—of which he had complained so bitterly—became a thing of the past.

In the late eighties the number of the "sympathizers" and the "interested" became too great. Tolstoy's house in Khamovnichesky Lane was besieged by visitors. The great writer's popularity had spread over the entire world. Everybody wanted to see him. With superhuman energy, the Countess kept a continuous open house. Her husband's popularity delighted her. She would have been happier if she could have confined the guests to her drawing room and limited them to prominent people, foreign visitors, and social acquaintances. But for some time a crowd of "dark ones" had been pouring irresistibly into Tolstoy's study. Scientists without names, young writers, students, pupils from religious seminaries, workmen, peasants who belonged to the various independent religious sects, "Tolstoyans" in Russian blouses and with long beards—all of them conquered their reticence and embarrassment, rang the bell at the magic door, and were shown by polite menservants through the back rooms and halls to the study of the "teacher." Communion with his fellow men occupied a prominent place in Tolstoy's program and was a martyrdom in itself. The people who gathered in Tolstoy's room were so variously motivated that only his exceptional tact could keep the constant seething of ideas and spiritual interests within peaceful bounds. Some of the more outspoken "Tolstoyans" at times openly attacked him for the inconsistency between his ideals and his mode of life. On such occasions Tolstoy rose to his full height, and with eyes sparkling insisted that the most important thing of all was to be on good terms with the people around him, and if to accomplish this he had to continue living in the old way, he was prepared to sacrifice his peace of mind.

"But what if it should become necessary to the peace of mind of those around me for me to take part in a robbery?" someone asked him indignantly.

Endless arguments of a different nature arose at the tea table over which the Countess presided. There Tolstoy had to defend his point of view on art, science, and religion against the generally accepted opinions of the scientists and thinkers of the day. His arguments with the philosopher Vladimir Soloviev were especially warm.

Tolstoy's mental energy was great, but these constant encounters tired him. At times he escaped the city noises to some friend's quiet country retreat, or most frequently to Yasnaya Polyana. This last journey of about one hundred and thirty miles he sometimes made on foot with one or two of his friends whom he liked for companions. A nameless old man, dressed in peasant clothes, with a rough stick in his hand, walked down the road, making new acquaintances, and talking endlessly with the people he met. The entire world of God opened before him, far beyond the limit of the conventions within which the great writer, Count Tolstoy, was forced to live. These journeys, which brought peace and quiet to his soul, frequently furnished unexpected and beautiful material to the artist within him.

Often he traveled third-class on the railroad. These trips to Yasnaya Polyana, which he called "baths in country life," became absolutely necessary to him. During the winter he usually escaped from Moscow every two months. When he emerged from the coach at the station and listened to the stillness of a village winter night, he experienced a feeling akin to ecstasy. Over the forest, Orion and Sirius shone in the starry skies, fluffy snow fell silently among the trees and he sensed close to him the gentle horse, the gentle air, the gentle Michael who came to meet him at the train, and above all, the gentleness of God.

In the country he arranged his life to suit himself and he often felt "unbearably well."

The Countess wrote to him: "Yesterday I received your first letter. I feel sad. I see that you have stayed in Yasnaya Polyana to play the part of some Robinson Crusoe, and not for the sake of your creative work, which I treasure more than anything else in life. You have dismissed Adrian, who was anxious to stay, you have dismissed the cook, who was happy because he was working for his pension, and from morning to night you do heavy manual labor, which in ordinary life is the lot of only young men and women. You would serve a more useful purpose if you were living with your children. You say that to live as you are living is in accordance with your convictions and that it makes you happy. That is a different matter, and I can only say, be happy; but I cannot help a regret that such a mind should be wasted on cutting wood, heating samovars, and making shoes, all of which is fine as a hobby, or as a change, but not as a profession. Enough of this! If I had not written as I have, I should have been bitter, but now I am gay and I will console myself with the old saying, 'What matter how a child plays, as long as he is happy?' "

On the same day she added: "Suddenly I saw you very clearly, and I felt an overwhelming tenderness for you. You have something exceptionally glowing, kind, naïve, and determined about you, and it shines with that special light—your sympathy for others and your insight into their souls."

In "simplifying" his life, Tolstoy one by one gave up all his pleasures. Hunting, his favorite relaxation, was given up in 1884. Three years later, he organized a temperance society, became a member, and took the pledge. At the same time he became a vegetarian. In 1888 he gave up tobacco.

3

In the summer of 1886 Tolstoy was bringing in a load of hay. He struck his leg against the side of the wagon but paid no attention to the bruise and continued to work for several days. The result was an infection accompanied by fever. He had to stay in bed. The doctor diagnosed an inflammation around the bone, with danger of general blood poisoning. The illness kept Tolstoy in bed for some time. In October Alexander Stakhovich came for a visit to Yasnaya Polyana. He held a high position at court, was a wealthy man of note, and had an unusual love of the theater and a remarkable dramatic talent. He read aloud exceptionally well. To entertain his sick host, Stakhovich read him Ostrovsky's dramas and comedies. Three weeks later, on his return journey from his country estate to Petersburg, he again stopped at Yasnaya Polyana. Tolstoy was much better. He was able to walk on crutches, and spent his time in an armchair in the drawing room.

To his guest he said, "I am glad you came. Your reading aroused me. After you left I wrote a play."

This was *The Power of Darkness*. During the preceding years, while he was rubbing shoulders with the plain people, Tolstoy had absorbed their psychology, their characters, and their language. He had made lengthy entries in his notebook. About a year before, Davidov, the district attorney for the Province of Tula, had told him among other stories about a case of child murder. The criminal, a peasant, had made a public confession.

Tolstoy not only put down the story in great detail, but twice went to see the murderer in prison. Later, during his illness, he suddenly felt that the characters in this tragedy of peasant life had become alive in his mind. Without being too serious about it, he began to work. He was too uncomfortable to write and dictated most of it. Glowing with delight, the Countess took down his words. She had not taken part in her husband's work for some time. She refused to copy his religious articles, saying that she had "resigned." But now she was cheerfully taking his dictation, and as in the old days making clean copies at night. She even wrote in her diary, "I will be careful and attentive with Lev, in order to preserve him for the work I love so much."

Within two and a half weeks the play was completed. The Countess made a final copy, and that evening Stakhovich read it aloud to the peasants who had been invited to hear it. About forty of them came and listened in silence. Only the pantry boy expressed his delight with noisy laughter.

The reading came to an end. Tolstoy turned to his favorite pupil, a middle-aged peasant, and asked, "How do you like it?"

The peasant answered, "I don't know what to say, Count. . . .

At first Mikita managed things pretty well, but in the end he slipped up."

This crushing answer caused Tolstoy a deep mental depression. He still held one of the essential factors in a work of art to be its universality and its meaning to the plain people.

The play was banned by the censors, for the stage as well as for publication.

But Tolstoy's friends decided to exercise their influence on his behalf. With ever improving mastery Stakhovich read *The Power of Darkness* in the fashionable salons of Petersburg. Everywhere the readings met with great success. Finally, on January 27, 1887, Alexander III expressed a desire to hear the play. The stage was set in Count Vorontsov's palace for Stakhovich to read the play before the entire imperial family.

Alexander III walked over to the table, picked up the manuscript, and said to Stakhovich, "This has been on my desk for a whole week. I could not find time to read it. Please read it without any omissions."

The reading began. The Tsar meticulously jotted down the list of characters on a piece of paper. Between the acts the men went out to smoke. All the conversation was centered on the play. The Tsar said about Mitrich, "The soldier is always so well portrayed by Tolstoy."

After the scene between Mitrich and Anyutka, Grand Duke Vladimir said to Stakhovich, "Even the sun has spots, and that is the only reason I permit myself to point out that this scene has a false note. Everything Mitrich says about women is true, but the words belong to Count Tolstoy and not to an old soldier. I cannot visualize this long philosophic monologue as a conversation between an old man and a young peasant girl."

The Tsar walked over to his brother and said, "You are wrong. Mitrich's words are perfectly natural under the circumstances, and are not monologues by the author. Anna had involuntarily started him on the subject, and under the impact of the horrible night and of everything that has happened behind the scene, Mitrich merely thinks aloud. Old people who put their sad thoughts about women and their fate into words often behave like that. In this instance he talks without paying any attention to his ten-year-old listener."

At the conclusion of the fifth act, everyone remained silent for a long time, waiting for the Tsar to speak. At last he said, "A marvelous piece of work!"

These five words unsealed everyone's lips. Conversation buzzed. On all sides were heard delighted exclamations: "Marvelous! Marvelous! . . ."

Under the pressure brought by society the censors were forced to relent, and permission for publication was given.

When *The Power of Darkness* appeared in print, two hundred and fifty thousand copies were sold within three days.

But when it came to producing the play, all the influential reactionaries lined up against Tolstoy. Prince Meshchersky, a friend of the Tsar, and the editor of the *Grazhdanin,* foamed at the mouth denouncing the "filthy" play. Pobyedonostzev in a series of letters alternately demanded and begged the Tsar to suppress production. The cast was selected, the parts were learned, the costumes and settings ready, but Alexander III appeared in person at the dress rehearsal and, under the influence of his advisers, forbade the presentation of the "marvelous piece of work."

The Power of Darkness appeared on the stage in Russia for the first time only at the end of 1895.

Deeply touched and delighted by the exceptional success of her husband's new creation, the Countess wrote to him, "How I wish that I could raise you even higher, so that the people would feel that they need wings to reach you, so that they would be touched when they read your books, so that what you write would not offend anyone but would make people better, and so that your books would retain their timeliness and character forever."

Tolstoy only laughed at such outpourings. He was much surprised at his tremendous success. He had simply written a play to be presented at fairs and in the village theaters. Jokingly he said, "If I had known they would like it so much, I should have tried to improve it."

His return to creative work brought about a reconciliation between husband and wife. The Countess became much less adamant. In 1886, after she had edited and published the twelfth volume of his works, Tolstoy in turn consented to look over old, unfinished material he had put aside: *In the Days of Serfdom,* which he had begun in the sixties, and *The Death of Ivan Ilyitch.*

In the spring of 1889, while he was visiting friends in the country, Tolstoy outlined a light comedy, *They Found a Way.* His eldest daughter persuaded her father to let her have the play for an amateur presentation at Yasnaya Polyana. Finding himself involved in what he called a "genteel fancy," Tolstoy became interested and put the final touches on the play in the midst of the incredible excitement that reigned in Yasnaya Polyana in December, 1889, as the rehearsals were getting under way. The final version was called *Fruits of Enlightenment.* The performance was a tremendous success, and the Russian public was presented with one of its favorite comedies.

On March 31, 1888, Tolstoy's last child was born—a son—Ivan.

4

The Kreutzer Sonata was begun in 1887. The final title had no connection with the original draft, in which Mrs. Posdnishev's seducer was a painter, not a musician. The husband catches them at the scene of their crime. The Countess felt that this scene was written in the style of Zola and she disliked it intensely. She tried to persuade Tolstoy that it was "disgusting," that there was no need for it, that the important thing was the husband's revenge, not the realism of the scene itself.

Tolstoy frowned and listened to her remarks with apparent displeasure. Evidently he resented it whenever anyone interfered with his conception of a story.

Probably that was the reason why he put the story aside and returned to the subject only two years later. The Tolstoys were having an evening at home. Among the guests were the famous painter Repin and the actor Andreyev-Burlak—a remarkable raconteur and reader. Count Sergei, Tolstoy's eldest son and a splendid musician, played the Kreutzer Sonata with the violinist Lassoto. As usual, it made a tremendous impression on Tolstoy. He said to Repin, "You must illustrate the Kreutzer Sonata, I will write a story, and Andreyev-Burlak shall read it."

Repin never attempted to carry out this project. Andreyev-Burlak died soon afterward. Tolstoy went back to his manuscript of 1887, and changed Mrs. Posdnishev's seducer from a painter to a musician.

Toward the end of August, 1889, the author was reading *The Kreutzer Sonata* to his guests in Yasnaya Polyana, while he continued to work on it.

The fate of this story was the same as the fate of everything he had written in his later years. The censors barred it from publication, but it was passed around in an endless number of lithographed, hectographed, and handwritten copies. People gathered in private homes in Petersburg and Moscow for the special purpose of reading the story that had caused such a furor. The critic Strakhov wrote to the author, "You must be aware that all through the winter your story was the only subject of conversation, and that when people met the custom was to ask, 'Have you read *The Kreutzer Sonata?*' instead of the usual, 'How are you?' "

Discussing the literary merit of the story, Strakhov said that he believed Tolstoy had never written anything stronger, but, he added, neither had he written anything more depressing.

Finally the Countess succeeded in personally presenting a petition to Alexander III and in securing permission to include the story in Tolstoy's complete works. On Chertkov's advice and in response to many requests, Tolstoy wrote the famous Epilogue.

Was *The Kreutzer Sonata* in any way a reflection of Tolstoy's private life in 1887?

In his diaries the following entry occurs:

"Many of the thoughts that I have expressed recently are not mine but belong to people who sympathize with my ideas and who come to me with their questions, surmises, thoughts, and plans. The basic thought, or, to be more exact, the feeling behind *The Kreutzer Sonata* belongs to a Slav woman who wrote me a letter, amusing in form, but significant in content, about the enslavement of women through sexual desire. Later she called on me and made a deep impression. The thought that Matthew's words about looking with desire at a woman refer not only to other men's wives, but to one's own as well, was expressed by an Englishman who wrote to me about it. The origin of many other ideas was similar."

In a letter to Prince Khilkov, Tolstoy wrote, "I was delighted to learn that you approve of *The Kreutzer Sonata*. When I fully understood them, the thoughts expressed in it were strange and unexpected to me. At times, I think that I hold such opinions only because I am old, and that is why opinions of people like you are so important to me."

Such admissions are interesting and valuable, but the fact remains that later Tolstoy was surprised by the "harsh, cold animosity" in family relations which permeates *The Kreutzer Sonata*.

The Countess hated the story. She was afraid that ugly gossip was being spread in connection with it and that people assumed Tolstoy had experienced the jealousy he so vividly described in his story. The Countess decided that she must clear her "reputation in the eyes of the children." She wrote an autobiographical novel, which she called *Whose Fault?* Her friends persuaded her not to publish it. While in *The Kreutzer Sonata* both husband and wife are blamed for the family differences, in the Countess's novel the husband is blamed for everything. The chief character in her novel is Prince Prozorovsky. After a stormy youth he marries, at thirty-five, the eighteen-year-old Anna. In drawing the girl's portrait the Countess was generous. Anna is the ideal girl: pure, gay, noble, and religious. Prince Prozorovsky, on the contrary, is a rough, sensual animal. When he walks behind his fiancée in the garden, he stares hungrily at her hips and mentally undresses her. After the wedding the pair leave in a coach, and in the darkness the animal Prozorovsky commits the act for which Anna is unprepared and which seems disgusting to her. The sensuous love of her husband fails to satisfy Anna. A sick dilettante painter appears on the scene and lays his romantic love at Anna's feet. In a fit of rage the husband, a jealous animal, murders his pure and innocent wife.

No matter what their origin, the moods and thoughts in *The Kreutzer Sonata* speak for themselves. Even if they had originated with someone else, the process of digesting and expressing them was certain to leave a residue in the author.

In *War and Peace*, not long before his death Prince Andrew Bolkonsky says to his friend, "Oh, my friend, of late I find it difficult to live! I see that I have begun to understand too much. No man should ever taste the fruit from the tree of knowledge."

In *The Kreutzer Sonata*, "understanding too much" was partly a reaction from the last reconciliation between Tolstoy and his wife.

The story *Devil* was written in 1889 and did not appear in print during the author's life. In reading it, it is useless to look for autobiographical material in the hero's unfaithfulness to his young wife. Physically the Tolstoys always remained true to each other. In September, 1887, Tolstoy told Biryukov, with whom he was very frank, "Nothing is more pleasant than the realization that I and my wife have never been unfaithful and that we have lived a clean and honest family life."

In 1901, when Tolstoy was severely ill, the Countess wrote, "At night I sit or lie by his side and I long to tell him that he is dear to me and that I never have loved anyone as I love him. If on the surface, through some unfortunate misunderstanding, I am at fault before him, I can say that inside me a solemn, strong love for him alone is firmly rooted and that I have never been unfaithful to him with as much as a single move of my little finger. I cannot tell him anything because I must not excite him. I have to think in silence about the results of thirty years of our married life, which actually was happy and clean, though I feel guilty at times because we were not happy to the fullest extent."

Some autobiographical material unquestionably is present in

the plot of *Devil*. Tolstoy admitted this, but he referred to an affair with a married peasant woman prior to his own marriage. One other important element is present in the story: the strength of habit due to physical proximity—a factor that was affecting Tolstoy's emotions in 1887 and which led to the sharp reaction in *The Kreutzer Sonata*.

On September 23, 1887, the Tolstoys celebrated their silver anniversary. Numerous friends and relatives gathered in Yasnaya Polyana for the occasion.

Looking back over twenty-five years of married life, Tolstoy was content to write only a few words in his diary: "Things could have been better."

Chapter Nine

DURING the nineties and the first decade of the twentieth century Tolstoy was working on a play called *The Light Shines Even in the Dark*. In it the drama of the author's life was disclosed without any attempt to disguise its autobiographical character. A wealthy landowner, Sarintsev, experiences a spiritual awakening and is consumed by a desire to conform his life to the teachings of Christ. His wife tries to protect the family fortunes and to defend established traditions. They even use the exact words that had been used by Tolstoy and the Countess. Only one trait distinguishes Sarintsev and his wife from the Tolstoys: the leading characters in the play are very considerate and willing to give in. In Sarintsev the desire not to upset the life of the family and not to deaden the love of one's neighbors overcomes the stern call of duty almost without a struggle.

But even this detail coincides to some extent with Tolstoy's own experiences.

The Countess, in her autobiography, seems at a loss: "I cannot decide when we began to part ways. And how or why? . . . I lacked the strength to follow his teachings, but our personal relations remained unchanged. We loved each other just as much, and it was just as difficult for us to part." The surprised tone is both sincere and understandable. During the nineties, Tolstoy wrote about three hundred letters to his wife. They all exude friendliness, consideration, and concern. Perhaps most of them lack the old warm feeling, but even in this respect there are exceptions.

On October 25, 1895, he wrote, "I wanted to write you, dear friend, on the very day of your departure, while the feeling that I experienced was still fresh, but a day and a half have elapsed, and I am only now settling down at my desk. The feeling that I experienced was one of peculiar sympathy, pity, and new love for you—of a love that transplanted me into you and made me feel what you feel. This sensation is so holy and so beautiful that I should not speak about it, but I know that you will be happy to hear this and I know that it will not disappear merely because I mention it. On the contrary, since I began writing you, the sensation is more real than ever. This sensation of ours is as strange as evening twilight. Only occasional clouds of your disagreements with me or of mine with you obscure the light. I always hope that they will disappear before night, and that the sunset will be bright and clear."

Spring came, and in May, Tolstoy's letters to his wife became even more tender; he asked her to read them "by yourself."

"How have you reached your destination, and how are you getting along, dear friend? Your visit made such a strong, wholesome, good impression on me—perhaps even too good—because I miss you that much more. My awakening and your appearance is one of the gayest and most vivid experiences I have ever had, and this when I am sixty-nine and you—fifty-three!"

This wave of tenderness came in the wake of some special circumstances. At the end of February, 1895, Ivan, Tolstoy's seven-year-old son, died of scarlet fever. Tolstoy had loved the boy dearly and had hoped that he would "continue God's work" after him. The mother's grief was inconsolable.

Tolstoy asked, "Why must children die? I have reached the conclusion that the only purpose in the life of every man is to strengthen love within himself, and by strengthening it within himself, to infect other people with it, thus strengthening love in them. . . . He [Ivan] lived so that he could strengthen love within himself; so that he would grow in love, as it was advocated by the One who sent him; and so that when he left life and returned to the One who is love, he could leave the love that had grown in him to us, to unite us. We have never been closer to each other than we are now, and never before have I felt in

Sonya or in myself such a need for love and such a revulsion from evil and from disagreement. I have never loved Sonya as much as I love her now."

There were other circumstances that helped their reconciliation, but old differences persisted.

In the Countess's mind their relations consisted almost entirely of their care for their mutual physical well-being, of worry about one another when they were separated, and of tenderness and friendliness in their letters. All this actually never changed.

Their sharp and harsh daily encounters, which were so minimized in Tolstoy's autobiographical play, were to the Countess more or less a natural part of married life. But in Tolstoy's soul these encounters were shaking and destroying the very foundations of habit and the last vestiges of love.

He could not forgive his wife for her hostility to his ideas. Even if she was unable to understand the "truth," still she should have trusted him and followed him for the sake of their love. Instead, she not only continued a way of life that he condemned, but (according to his views) she was also destroying their children. Inwardly he was inclined to blame her for all the inconsistencies of his life. He repaid her "lack of understanding" with bitter jokes and sarcasms. In his diaries, in his letters, in his conversations with his friends, he frequently made accusations that came back to her.

This kept the Countess in an antagonistic state of mind.

Her great energy and practical abilities, which she had clearly demonstrated at a critical point, gave her confidence and self-assurance. She definitely became the head of the family. Tolstoy seemed incapable of insisting on his views or of leaving. He felt that he was guilty before himself, before his teachings, and before his family, whose needs no longer interested him. His indecision made her more confident than ever. She even attempted to interfere in his relations with the public and made statements that were distasteful to him. Without his knowledge, and directly contrary to his wishes, public statements appeared over his name.

Occasionally he had to disentangle himself from embarrassing situations in which he had been placed by the tactlessness of his wife.

2

All this does not mean that Tolstoy's prestige within the family was any the less. He was greatly loved; and besides, the Countess, who became more and more outspoken in her opinions and arguments, realized that she could not go beyond certain limits. Losing Tolstoy would have meant to her and to her family the loss of a position that they enjoyed on the strength of his world-wide popularity. For his part Tolstoy, too, worked persistently on himself. He deliberately tried to soften the violence of his reactions, and to control himself. The way in which the family lived depressed him and he persisted in his complaints and accusations, though he tried to be calm and reasonable. But frequently his discontent overpowered his will and produced terrific explosions.

His desire to relinquish his copyrights is a good example. After his spiritual transformation, Tolstoy was tortured by the thought that he was being paid for what he wrote. He compared paying an author to prostitution and to a liquor monopoly. In the meantime, in the energetic hands of the Countess the sales of his works became the source of a large income. This subject was a cause of constant quarrels. The Countess definitely refused to accept her husband's views. His books constituted the family's wealth, and without them they could not exist. Giving in as easily as the hero of his play, Sarintsev, Tolstoy tried to find a compromise. He tried to persuade her to permit the free distribution of at least those of his works which were written after 1881, the year of his "spiritual rebirth." This situation came to a head in July, 1891. Just as in most violent family scenes, inexcusable things were said. The Countess decided to end it all. She rushed out of the house and ran toward the railroad, intending to throw herself under a train. Accidentally she met her brother-in-law Kuzminsky, who was startled by her appearance and her excited state. Having learned everything from her, he succeeded in calming her and in bringing her home.

Tolstoy bided his time; but soon after, he raised the question again. He asked his wife to announce in the newspapers a list of those of his works which anyone might publish. He suggested that she do this in her own name, or, failing that, that she do it over his signature. Cautiously he added, "But if you don't like this, don't do it. I am not too eager about it. An announcement like that has its good and its bad sides."

The Countess wrote, "I disagreed with this suggestion at the time, because I thought it unfair to deprive our large and by no means wealthy family."

In September, Tolstoy again raised the same question and again without results. At last he sent her the full text of a public announcement in which he relinquished all his rights in works written after 1881.

This time the announcement appeared in the papers without the Countess's consent.

The relations between the Countess and the peasants were also a frequent and important cause for disagreements between husband and wife. In accordance with her power of attorney, she managed her husband's estate. In protecting the property against individual peasants, she was forced to apply to the courts for help. She prosecuted peasants for trespass, for cutting timber, and for thefts. So long as the family owned land and operated a farm, this was inevitable; but when, as a result of the landowner's complaint, the guilty peasants were dragged to prison by the police, Tolstoy found himself in a difficult position and went through tragic moments. His appeals to his wife's sympathy seldom met with any response. Everyone felt that Tolstoy should at least be relieved of formal responsibility for the Countess's actions. There was talk in the family of a division of property.

Tolstoy definitely refused to own anything. He suggested that everything be handled as if he had died. His heirs were to divide everything among them. The estate was divided into ten equal shares and apportioned among the nine children and the Countess. The formal deed was signed on April 17, 1891.

Tolstoy's last resort in all family quarrels was a threat to leave home. His wife always countered with a threat to end her life.

But where and how could Tolstoy go? Could he become a nameless tramp? He had not had sufficient determination to take such a step even immediately after he had discovered the evangelical truth. He was a proud person. He liked to submit when a conductor in the third-class of a train, mistaking him for a peasant, pushed him around or when the servants drove him away from the doors of some prominent acquaintance. He even found it amusing. All he had to do was to give his right name and the most powerful came running down the stairs, trying to find suitable ways to show their esteem for the "old peasant" who had honored them with a visit. The position of a nameless tramp would be different. He would be threatened with prison, with exile, and with endless insults. The idea sounded attractive only in a daydream. No wonder his artistic sense would not allow him to finish his story about the transformation of Emperor Alexander I into the old tramp Feodor Kuzmich.

In the nineties Tolstoy had begun work on a remarkable novel called *Father Sergei*. His hero had achieved great fame; people from every corner of Russia came to him for spiritual assistance and consolation. As a result of many complex motives, many of which were taken from Tolstoy's own experiences, Father Sergei has an urge to escape his fame. For a long time he keeps peasant clothes hanging in his room, but he lacks the determination to take the final step. Only a great sin finally forces him to break away from his former life.

Sarintsev, in the play *The Light Shines Even in the Dark*, also has not the strength to escape the life to which he is accustomed.

Other considerations besides pride and fame held Tolstoy back.

Like every prophet, he felt an irresistible desire to teach people. He made many deprecatory references to this weakness in his *Confession*. After his spiritual rebirth this passion to teach became even stronger. Sympathetic friends insisted that God was speak-

ing through Tolstoy's lips. The tremendous spiritual powers of
the great writer were seeking ways to express themselves, and he
had a passionate desire within the limits of his life to preach everything he had felt and thought. If he were to lose himself among
nameless tramps, he had to cease being a prophet. His influence
would be limited only to a few people, whom he would meet
accidentally.

The life to which he was accustomed had a strong hold on him.
A seventy-year-old man found it difficult to break all the old
ties, and become a nameless tramp.

To leave in some other way? . . . To continue writing, to
keep his name and his position? . . . Tolstoy's sincerity told him
that such a compromise would mean only endless tortures for
himself and for his family, and a hopelessly false situation.

As he put it, he leaned toward the lesser of the two evils, and
remained as a "hanger-on with a wealthy family."

Excerpts, taken at random from his diaries, show that he suffered.

"Depressing, rotten! I find everything about the life that is
led around me revolting. At times I free myself from the depression and torture, and then I succumb to them again. . . .

"The greatest temptation in my position is living amid luxurious conditions, which I forced myself to accept in order not to
destroy love. I have reached a point when I am not certain
whether I continue to live in this way because I fear to destroy
love or because I have yielded to temptation. . . .

"I lead a dirty, rotten life with my children and I justify it
by the false fear of destroying love. Instead of sacrifices, instead
of an inspiring example, I lead a rotten, pharisaical life that is
contrary to the teachings of Christ. . . .

"I prayed that He would save me from this life and I am
praying again, and screaming with pain. . . . I have become
trapped, entangled. I cannot free myself, but I feel no hate for
myself—only for my way of living. . . ."

The pain that made him "scream" also made him want to leave

home regardless of consequences. Evidence discloses two such attempts, and very likely there were others.

On July 8, 1897, Tolstoy wrote a letter to his wife in which he said that he had decided to leave. "This decision has to be carried out." He thanked his wife for their thirty-five years of married life, and asked her to let him go of her own free will, not to look for him, not to miss him, and not to condemn him. He could no longer live as he had lived during the last sixteen years, at times fighting and irritating the family, "at others succumbing to the temptations of habit." But the chief reason was that, having reached his seventieth year, he wanted to go alone "into the forest" in order to devote his last years to God.

Tolstoy changed his mind and never mailed this letter. The Countess read it after his death.

On another occasion he made plans to leave in a year and asked help from one of his followers—a Finnish writer whom he had never seen.

But on the whole, during the nineties, he was inclined to consider an escape, not as a sacrifice, but as an unforgivable weakness. Beginning with the late eighties, Tolstoy had entered a new phase, or, as his biographers describe it, he reached a new and "higher stage in his religious and moral development."

3

While he was exulting over the newly discovered truth, the reformation of the world seemed a simple and easy matter. All that people had to do was to collect their thoughts, realize the senselessness and horror of their existence, and they would inevitably accept the way to salvation pointed out by Christ and interpreted in *What Do I Believe?* The road had been made clear to them by the Gospels, and even more so by the five commandments in the Sermon on the Mount. The reformation of the world was at hand, but it could not be brought about by words or theoretical teachings. People had to have examples of the simplicity and the happiness of true Christian life. But the ten-year period of waiting for the inevitable change was in vain. People obstinately turned away from the Kingdom of God on Earth. The instances of refusal to bear arms remained isolated, and those who, as a matter of religious principle, were brave enough to refuse were severely punished. One by one, Tolstoy's agricultural colonies fell apart. Tolstoy attempted to realize the Christian ideal in his own life; but in trying, he—as he expressed it—broke his hands.

A period of disappointment followed. The triumph of truth seemed further away than ever—certainly he never would see it in his lifetime.

Truth had to be tempered by worldly considerations, and compromises had to be found. There were moments when he became desperate and doubted his own teachings. In the meantime, within his soul, a constant, slow change was taking place. It produced unexpected results.

Once again Tolstoy's beliefs reached a new phase. He no longer defended the premises he had so warmly expounded in his *What Do I Believe?*

Deep down in his heart he was glad that he had "lived down" these opinions.

What was this newly discovered truth? Tolstoy's new faith shifted the concern of a Christian from the outward sphere, from the sphere of action, to an inward world—to self-improvement.

No one is expected to change the world in the name of truth. No one can realize truth even in his own life, no matter how much he wishes; but without worrying about the world, without worrying whether or not his example seems logical to other people, everyone, to the limit of his ability, can realize the truth in the eyes of God. In other words, everyone has to carry out His will. That is the love which should grow within the individual, and within the entire world. By letting love grow, by gathering everything lovable, man prepares to unite with God after death, prepares for eternal life.

Can Christianity be practiced?

No one should worry about that. The results of our actions are beyond our control. In his proud desire to reform the world, man inevitably meets obstacles that no one can foresee. Man finds it difficult to change even his own way of living. With every step he encounters incomprehensible inconsistencies. To break through them would inevitably mean resisting evil with force, thus breaking the commandment to love one's neighbors. Present life is too closely interwoven with past temptations and with past sins.

Man cannot accept Christian teachings as rules of conduct. If he were to try, Christianity would at once become unrealizable. Christianity is merely an ideal for which man should yearn. Living in accordance with Christian teachings is a movement toward Godlike perfection.

Our actions and the changes in the conditions of our lives are not dependent on ourselves. Man should even try to force himself to resign forever from any attempt to change outward circumstances. The consciousness and the acceptance of truth are what is important.

"If people could only understand that they should stop worrying about superficial social matters in which they are not free to act, and would devote a hundredth of the energy they expend on superficialities, to the things in which they have a free choice: being conscious of and accepting the truth that confronts them, and liberating themselves and others from the falsehood and duplicity that obscure the truth. If this were to happen, the false way of living that tortures people and threatens them with even more dire disasters would collapse without any effort or struggle, and the Kingdom of God, or at least the first step for which people are ready in their consciences, would become a reality."

Thus, teaching by action and example is superfluous.

"Man has to become accustomed to the thought that no matter how closely he follows Christ, there will be others who will not accept Christ and who will condemn him. . . .

"The Christian can achieve his purpose only by burning an inward light, which will serve as a beacon to other people. . . .

Our actions must have roots, and these roots lie in submitting to the will of God in our private lives, which have to be devoted to perfection and to the cultivation of love. . . ."

Tolstoy summed up: "If the transformation takes place within the soul, the transformation in the world will follow."

Purify yourself, carry the light of Christian truth within, exemplify the validity of Christianity, and of a sensible and happy life, under any circumstances—that is the best way to practice one's faith and to enlighten people. As soon as people become firm in their faith, as pure as doves, and as wise as serpents, they will overcome all obstacles without a struggle and the world will be reformed.

Individual self-improvement and love, under any imaginable circumstances, became Tolstoy's new tenets.

He no longer had any reason to leave the family that lived in a way contrary to his convictions.

His was a trial sent to him by God. The more difficult he found his position in the family, the oftener he heard accusations of insincerity because he continued to live amid wealth and pleasures, the more he had to learn to accept, to forgive, and to love.

Later, on July 2, 1908, he wrote in his diary, "If I had overheard someone tell about a man who lived in luxury, who squeezed what he could from the peasants and threw them into prison, who professed and preached Christianity while he gave away pennies, and who, whenever anything unpleasant had to be done, hid behind his wife's back, I would never have hesitated to call him a cad! That was what I needed to free me from worldly things, and to enable me to live for my soul."

4

"Self-improvement" had been the ideal of his youth, which underwent such severe scrutiny in *My Confession*. Now he was speaking of self-improvement with a definite purpose, but even the Christian understanding of life opened before him endless vistas for thought. In his childhood he had speculated until he had almost lost his mind. In his old age his fine dialectics at times lent remarkable meaning to his conception of self-improvement.

Love? . . . But whom and how to love? Could the human race be loved as such? Or could this be achieved only through God, after one had become conscious of love for the divine particle within oneself? Could one retain personal attachments in a world of Christian love? Was it possible to love one's enemies, or was it necessary to make friends of them first? He wrote, "You say that no one can love Herod. I don't know. But I know, and you know, that we must love him. I know, and you know, that if I fail to love him, I will hurt myself, that I cannot live fully, and that I must work on myself until I make it possible. I can imagine a man who has all his life been loved by everyone for his love, but who cannot force himself to love Herod, and I can imagine another man who exhausted his strength trying to learn to love Herod, and remained indifferent to those who loved him, who could not learn to love for twenty years but who in the twenty-first year succeeded, and made Herod love him and all the people. I cannot say which of the two is better."

In connection with obedience to the will of the Creator, innumerable other questions arose. Tolstoy tried to formulate answers:

"In my lucid moments I am inclined to believe that everything hinges on permitting love to assert itself within, and all that is necessary is to avoid temptations. As soon as the temptations are out of the way, love will assert itself, and will lead a man to act, whether through enlightening the world, or through taming and pacifying a spider. Everything is equally important."

Fortunately his ability to love, with which he was endowed by nature, in most instances led him past the fine theoretical points, and into the path of suffering humanity.

In the summer of 1891, Rayevsky, a landowner in the Province of Ryazan, and an old friend of the Tolstoys, came to Yasnaya Polyana. Central Russia was threatened with famine, and Rayevsky could not talk about anything else. Countess Alexandra Tolstoy was visiting Yasnaya Polyana at the same time and she has described the irritation with which Tolstoy listened to his guest. He contradicted Rayevsky's every word, insisted that all this was nonsense, and that if famine came, people had to submit to the will of God. Without paying any attention, Rayevsky continued to express his fears, while "Lev quietly developed his peculiar ideas, which made a very strange impression on his listeners."

In September the well-known writer Leskov wrote to Tolstoy, asking him what he thought should be done to relieve the suffering. Tolstoy answered that he would not participate in collecting donations for relief. In his opinion, good deeds were not a matter of giving bread to the hungry, but of loving equally those who were hungry and those who had enough to eat.

These theories could not endure in the face of grim reality. After two visits to the stricken area, Tolstoy suddenly borrowed five hundred rubles from the Countess, and with his two daughters went to the Province of Ryazan to aid Rayevsky, whose tales of famine he had scorned during the preceding summer. Rayevsky was at work already. Feeding stations for children and for old people were in operation and donations were coming in. The Countess published an appeal in the newspapers for help for the stricken people. Money, clothes, and volunteer workers from all over Russia and from abroad, especially from England, began to arrive at the Tolstoy home. Tolstoy wrote a series of brilliant articles, in which he took the opportunity to air his favorite theories. Some of these articles appeared only abroad.

The people who were closest to him and who worked with him, regretted his apparent inconsistencies and expressed their doubts in him: "How, after saying all he had about helping people with money, could he accept donations and distribute among the needy wealth that had been stolen from the poor?"

He was attacked continuously by the more consistent among his followers, and he joined them in denouncing his work.

All the while, through two severe winters, he was saving the people of four counties from famine; and in carrying on this work, he demonstrated a great deal of practical sense. The number of feeding stations reached two hundred and forty-six, and thirteen thousand adults and three thousand children were fed in them. He fed people twice a day and spent between ninety-five kopeks and one ruble thirty kopeks on each person every month. But he was not satisfied with this extensive undertaking. Through the midwinter months, when the people were freezing from lack of fuel, he arranged to supply the neediest families with wood. He took hundreds of starving horses from the peasants and arranged for feeding them. He procured large quantities of flax and bast, and distributed them among the population so that they could make linen and shoes. He organized milk stations for young children. In the spring he distributed potatoes and seed for planting among the needy peasants. When the time came for field work, he bought additional horses and distributed them. To the people who could still afford it, he sold flour and bread at very low prices.

This immense activity stirred Russian society. Feeding stations organized in accordance with the Tolstoy plan were opened all over Russia. During the famines of later years Tolstoy's example and his ways of rendering aid served as a pattern.

Toward the end of the nineteenth century circumstances forced Tolstoy to be inconsistent again. This time it was the problem of financial relief for the Dukhobors. Their teachings had much in common with Tolstoy's, and as a sect they were mercilessly persecuted by the Russian Government.

Tolstoy responded warmly to the fate of the Dukhobors. When, after a great deal of effort, the Tsar's permission for the emigration of eight thousand Dukhobors was finally secured, Tolstoy organized the collection of a fund to help them. As his contribution he reworked, finished, and sold his novel *Resurrection,* and donated all the profits from the first Russian and foreign editions to the Dukhobor fund.

These inexcusable "crimes" again drew a series of attacks from his followers. In answer to one of them he wrote:

"What you say is absolutely true. I have thought and still think, have felt and still feel, that it is evil and shameful to ask for material aid for people who are suffering for the sake of the truth. You will ask, why then have I joined Chertkov, Biryukov, and Tregubov in signing the appeal? I was opposed to it just as much as I was opposed to giving help in this way during the famine. But what can a man do when told that there are children, old people, and weak pregnant women who are suffering and that he can help them by speaking or acting? He has to speak or act. To consent means to be inconsistent with the expressed opinion that always and in every circumstance, true virtue lies in purifying one's own life of sin and in living not for oneself but for God, and that giving help with products of labor which were stolen from the people is a deceit, a pharisaical act, and an endorsement of the Pharisees. But not to consent means to refuse to speak or act in a way that would relieve the immediate suffering of the needy. Out of the weakness of my character I always choose the second alternative, though this decision tortures me."

In 1885 Tolstoy said to a writer who was visiting him, "Millions of Russians who can read stand before us openmouthed, like hungry blackbirds, and say: Gentlemen, writers, give us mental fare worthy of you and of us. Give us, who crave life, real literature and save us from commercial fare. Plain honest Russians deserve an effort on our part and we must respond to the appeal of their kind and truthful souls. I have thought a great deal about this and have decided to do as much as I can in this field."

This was the beginning of an entire series of beautiful folk legends and tales written by Tolstoy. He borrowed them everywhere: from the tales told by tramps, from the songs of the itinerant minstrels who visited him, and from the Lives of the Saints. The restraint, the brevity, the simplicity, and the artistic beauty of these fine creations are remarkable.

Tolstoy was not satisfied merely with creating examples of true folk literature. He wanted quantities of it to reach the peasantry. In those days books were sold to the people by itinerant traders who traveled from village to village, carrying their wares in wicker baskets. For this reason the books they sold were nicknamed "wicker literature." Popular illustrated books cost from one to one and a half kopeks, but in most instances the writing was poor and the books very badly manufactured.

Tolstoy approached one of the larger publishers of "wicker literature" and suggested that his books be gradually replaced by something more worth while. The prices and manner of distribution were to remain unchanged. The publisher consented. At Tolstoy's suggestion, the company "Posrednik" was organized. The attempt to draw the important literary figures into this work was successful. Tolstoy took a warm and active part in the editorial end of the work. For ten years he guided the selection of books, outlined the subjects, and corrected, reworked, and edited the manuscripts that came in. Because of strict censorship his work was, as he expressed it, like tight-rope walking. Without a large operating capital, conducting business on a large scale was difficult, and the company was constantly in need of funds. Tolstoy assisted generously with money and by assigning the rights to his books, the first editions of which always brought tremendous profits. In this way millions of good books, well-manufactured and well-illustrated, reached the poorer people.

Other money that, in theory, he damned was at Tolstoy's disposal. His plays were presented on the stages of the state theaters. As was the custom, a certain percentage of the receipts was credited to the author's account. Though he had refused to accept any royalties, the Countess had countermanded his orders, and about two or three thousand rubles yearly were placed to his credit. This was his pocket money, and he spent it entirely on the charity that he so greatly condemned.

He also helped in other ways. He was always pleading on someone's behalf. He sent sick people into town with letters to the physicians he knew. His influential acquaintances—lawyers especially—were swamped with his appeals for aid to peasants who needed protection. His particular zeal and sympathy were aroused on behalf of conscientious objectors and of people who were subjected to government persecution as members of various religious sects. No amount of effort was too much for Tolstoy, and in many instances he wrote directly to the Tsar.

In addition, he saw a constant stream of people who came to him for advice, and attended to a voluminous correspondence, in which he made it a rule not to overlook a single letter that he thought deserving of an answer.

And he still found time for his literary work. During the decade 1890 to 1899 he wrote dozens of articles, some of which assumed major proportions, such as *What is Art?* and *The King-dom of God Is Within You.* Tolstoy's original opinions on art are well known. *The Kingdom of God Is Within You* was planned as an article against compulsory military service. The article grew into a large book presenting the basic theories of Christian anarchism. It summarized Tolstoy's current under-standing of Christianity, on the strength of which he denounced any form of government or of organized religion, both of which, he felt, depended entirely on force that was superfluous in an enlightened age.

During the same period, Tolstoy wrote over a dozen other works, among which *Resurrection, Father Sergei,* and *Master and Servant* were particularly successful.

In theory, the effort to "learn to love King Herod" or to "tame a spider" seemed as important to Tolstoy as the enlighten-ment of the world, or any other activity on behalf of humanity in general.

In practice, he always rushed with characteristic warmth to the rescue of the needy. Whenever the necessity arose, he forgot about spiders and Herod, and deliberately acted in a manner contrary to his own theories. The narrowness of his teachings was foreign to him. He had no fear of being inconsistent, and dis-missed the protests of his disciples.

The Light Shines Even in the Dark remained unfinished. As far as can be deduced from the outline of the fifth act, Tolstoy intended to show that the light of the neo-Christian teachings proved victorious over the darkness of contemporary materialistic life. But he found it difficult to make his point. The hero of his play perishes rather ingloriously. Everything around him collapses. All that remains at the time of his death is the pleasant realization that "the deception of the church has been broken, and life has acquired a new meaning."

In actual life Tolstoy reacted differently to circumstances. In the dark labyrinth of his changeable philosophies his responsive heart always served as a beacon.

That is the light—the light of warm, generous work for the sake of humanity—which lighted and still lights the dark path of human life.

Chapter Ten

ONE DAY in the middle nineties the Countess was talking to the tutor of her younger sons. *The Kreutzer Sonata* was mentioned, and they began to discuss relations between men and women. Tolstoy entered the room and said:

"So that's the question that interests you? I believe that people who produce novels that end with a wedding, as if it were a happy ending and there were nothing further to write about, are spreading a lot of nonsense. If there has to be a comparison, marriage should be compared to a funeral, and not to a birthday. A man has been walking alone, suddenly two hundred pounds are tied to his shoulders, and he is supposed to enjoy it. How can there be any question? When I am walking alone, I am free. When my foot is shackled to a woman's foot, she will drag behind me and get in my way."

"Then why did you marry?" the Countess asked.

"I had no idea of it then."

"All you are saying is that you are always changing your opinions."

"Every man should strive for perfection. Personally, I cannot complain about my family life. On the contrary, my family life has turned out very happily. I know many people who have come together and live well with one another. Still, marriage is not a holiday! Two people come together to get in each other's way."

"I think that they come together to help each other."

"How can they help each other? Two people who are strangers come together and remain strangers all their lives. Some people compare a husband and a wife to parallel lines. Why parallel? I have always said that to find among a great number of crossing lines two that are parallel is just as difficult as it is to find two similar natures. Marriage is more like two crossing lines.

As soon as they cross, they continue to diverge. If anyone wants to marry, he certainly should marry. Perhaps he will be able to arrange his life happily, but he must realize that he will be handicapped, and he should concentrate all his efforts on making their mutual existence as happy as possible."

Toward the end of 1899, Tolstoy wrote in his diary, "The chief cause of unhappiness in married life is that people have been taught to think that marriage means happiness. The incentive for marriage is sex attraction, which takes the form of promises and hopes of happiness—a view supported by public opinion and by literature. But marriage cannot cause happiness. Instead, it always means torture, with which man has to pay for satisfying his sex urge. These tortures are lack of freedom, servility, satiety, revulsion, all sorts of moral and physical defects in one's mate, which one is forced to endure, such as temper, stupidity, dishonesty, vanity, drunkenness, laziness, greed, cupidity, and immorality—all defects that it is much more difficult to endure in others than in oneself and which make one suffer as if they were one's own—and such physical imperfections as ugliness, slovenliness, odors, diseases, insanity, and many others that are even more unbearable. All of them, or at least some of them, are always present, and everyone has to face them. Everything that recompenses for them—thoughtfulness, satisfaction, help—is taken for granted; all the shortcomings are considered as something superfluous, and the more happiness people expect of marriage, the more they suffer. The main reason is that people expect the impossible, and are not prepared for the usual. Escape from torture lies not in expecting happiness, but in anticipating the worst, and in being prepared to bear it. If a man expects everything mentioned in the opening of *A Thousand and One Nights*, if a man expects drunkenness, stench, and revolting diseases, then he may overlook such minor defects as stubbornness, duplicity, and even drunkenness, cease suffering, and be happy in the realization that worse possible things—insanity, cancer, and whatever else is mentioned in *A Thousand and One Nights*—

are absent. Such a state of mind will make a man really appreciate everything good."

As the years went by, Tolstoy voiced his opinions on women more and more frequently. These opinions were not flattering. He delivered his philippics to friends and pupils, and at times in the presence of ladies. He even went further and hinted that his opinions were based on his experiences with his wife and daughters.

He said, "If men knew women as husbands know their wives, they would never talk seriously to them about anything."

On July 16, 1901, he wrote in his diary, "Only husbands learn to know their wives and only when it is too late. Only husbands see behind the curtains. That is why Lessing insisted that all husbands say: There is only one bad woman, and she is my wife. In the presence of others, women—especially when they are young—pretend so skillfully that no one can see them as they are."

The association with his daughters should have modified his opinions of women. Tolstoy's three daughters displayed an unwavering attachment for him. All three to a lesser or greater degree submitted to his authority, willingly participated in his spiritual life, and actively helped with his extensive correspondence.

The five sons drew themselves further away from his teachings. Sergei and Ilya, the two eldest, who had grown up under the spell of the Tolstoy of the old days, were attached to their father. The other three were not as close to him. They had grown up during the period of depressing quarrels in the family, and their sympathies were with their mother.

As time went on, the family became smaller. Tolstoy's opinions of women failed to prevent his sons' early marriages: the last one was married in 1901. After they were married, they moved away and only occasionally came to visit in Yasnaya Polyana.

Even the daughters, who shared Tolstoy's opinions, were married in the course of time: Mary to Prince Obolensky in 1897, and Tatyana to M. S. Sukhotin in 1899.

Tolstoy was left with his wife and youngest daughter.

The 1900's were a period of frequent and severe illnesses for the aging Tolstoy. In 1901 he was so weak that a family council decided to follow the advice of physicians and take him to the southern coast of the Crimea for the winter. Countess Panin, as soon as she heard the news, placed her beautiful villa, Gaspra, at the family's disposal. There Tolstoy went through three consecutive serious illnesses. At times death seemed inevitable. The physicians lost all hope, but his remarkably strong constitution, the exceptional efforts of physicians who gathered from everywhere, and the altogether extraordinary care saved Tolstoy. During that trying winter Tolstoy was surrounded by the tender attention and love of his entire family. The Countess never slept at night and was at his bedside every minute. His sons, his daughters, and his friends gathered at Gaspra, remained for long periods, and took their turns at the sick man's bedside.

Everyone agreed that, while Tolstoy hovered between life and death, he was extremely patient, kind, and gentle with those around him.

While they were still in Yasnaya Polyana, the Countess had written in her diary:

"This morning, while I was putting a poultice on his chest, he looked at me attentively, began to cry, and said, 'Thank you, Sonya! . . . Please never think that I am not grateful, or that I have no love for you. . . .' His voice broke in a sob, I kissed his dear hands, which I know so well, and told him how happy I was to nurse him, how guilty I felt because I had not given him sufficient happiness and that he should forgive me for not giving him something that I did not know how to give. We were both in tears as we embraced. This is what my soul has been craving for so long. This is a serious, deep realization of our closeness during the thirty-nine years we have spent together. . . . Everything that interrupted it at times was an intrusion from outside, and nothing ever affected the firm, inner ties of the beautiful love within us. . . ."

After the Crimean illness the family spent all their time in

Yasnaya Polyana. The children's education was no longer a consideration. The Countess paid occasional visits to Moscow on business.

The differences between husband and wife never ceased. Warm, human love between the Countess and Tolstoy was lacking. As one part of his theory, he even worked consciously to rid himself of all personal attachments; his ideal was to love all people equally, and especially his enemies. Singling out individuals, no matter how close to him, was a sin, which must be overcome. This, again, was theory. In real, everyday life he remained human, and having lost his love for his wife, he failed to treat her always in a true Christian spirit. Frequently he became excited, angry, and abusive.

The Countess cherished what was left of her attachment for him. She looked after him, she worried constantly about his physical condition, and she became flustered and blushed at the least attention from him. With all her soul, she hated Tolstoy's teachings. They interfered with her love and threatened the material security of her family; they robbed her of the soul of the man she loved, and erected a barrier between them. Alone among a crowd of Tolstoy's admirers, she became desperate, and at the first mention of Tolstoy's theories felt that she had to contradict them. Tolstoy's sarcasms, his protests, and his references to family life, marriage, and women, provoked her to point out the inconsistencies in his theories and to ridicule them, regardless of who was present. At the same time her self-assurance, about which Tolstoy had complained even in the early years of their marriage, continued to grow. Her utter contempt for the ideas of her husband shocked his admiring followers and could not fail to have an effect on him. He became silent, and frequently disappeared into his room, but occasionally he exploded, and made a scene.

2

During the intervals between his illnesses, though he was getting old, Tolstoy felt sufficiently active to ride daily on horseback ten, fifteen, or even twenty miles. He always chose unknown paths through the woods, descended into hollows, made his horse jump high barriers, climbed almost vertical hills, and generally surprised his younger companions by his energy. In Moscow during the nineties he even took indoor bicycle lessons, quickly acquired the technique, and for a time went on long bicycle trips.

But age made itself felt. He was no longer able to perform manual labor. His remarkable capacity for literary work was noticeably on the wane. In the evenings he could only read, play chess, and listen to music. Even so, during the last ten years of his life he produced about forty articles on philosophical, religious, and sociological problems. Over thirty literary creations belong to the same period, and among them are such masterpieces as *The Living Corpse, The Light Shines Even in the Dark, Hadjii Murad, After the Ball,* and *Reminiscences of Childhood.*

In 1901 the seven metropolitans and bishops who made up the synod of the Russian Orthodox church pronounced the anathema on Tolstoy. As theologians, they were right in excommunicating him: he had been in opposition to the church for a long time. But their action only increased his popularity. At first he refused to answer and restrained the Countess from doing so. But she was anxious to fight for him and insisted. Her none-too-strong open letter to Metropolitan Antoni appeared in the newspapers.

Later Tolstoy answered the synod. He took the opportunity to set forth again the basic tenets of his faith. Among other things he said, "I began by loving my Orthodox faith more than my peace of mind, then I learned to love Christianity more than my church, now I love truth more than anything else."

This truth he had no intention of disavowing, or forcing on anyone, because "I have to live and die only with myself."

Such statements characterize the beginning of a new change

in Tolstoy's views and of a new phase of his inward development.

He found it difficult to preach anything any more, because he was gradually abandoning all dogmas. Even his belief in the special significance of Christianity weakened. He studied other religions and found similarities in all of them. This remarkable fact was explained by a learned rabbi with whom Tolstoy had studied the Talmud and the Prophets in the ancient Hebrew: "Tolstoy took from the texts only what he wanted. He regarded the rest with complete indifference."

Finding in all religions only the thoughts that were dear to him, Tolstoy finally decided that they were the only truths set forth by God, inasmuch as they suited everyone's conscience. Everything else led to discord and was the product of man's brain.

Thus the Gospel lost its special significance and Tolstoy's ardor for it cooled.

To be universal, religious thought must be very simple, and Tolstoy's religion was reduced to a few precepts. Obey the will of God who sent you here. You will unite with Him after your physical death. God's will is for people to love one another and to act toward others as they want others to act toward them.

Even these broad formulas failed to satisfy him. He wrote in his diary, "I once asked myself: What do I believe? Do I actually believe that the purpose of life is obeying the will of God, that He wants love and unity to grow within the individual and within the entire world, and that through this growth and through loving everything I am preparing myself for future life? Instinctively, I answered that I cannot believe anything so definite. What, then, do I believe? I answered in all sincerity, that I believe one must be good and humble, one must forgive and love. That much I believe with my entire being."

The search that had lasted for so many years was almost at an end. At times he doubted everything—even the existence of God. Even in theory he refused to accept the existence of God the creator, of God the thinker, or of God who could answer questions. To him God was infinite, God was everything—a boundless everything, of which he felt himself a part. Everything in him was close to God and he felt Him in everything.

This was so broad and vague that the question sometimes occurred to Tolstoy: Is it possible to get along altogether without God?

He wrote, "I began to think that it was possible and necessary to abandon this conception in order to unite with the Chinese, the Confucianists, the Buddhists, and our own atheists and agnostics. I thought that men should be satisfied with the realization and with the acceptance of the God within us, of the God who placed his divine spark in us, and without striving to accept God in general. Strangely enough, I at once felt bored, depressed, and frightened. I had no idea why, but I felt that I had suddenly fallen spiritually, and that I had been deprived of all joy and spiritual energy. Only then did I understand that this had happened because I had forsaken God. By thinking and guessing whether there is a God, I had rediscovered Him again."

Tolstoy wanted to lean on his faith in God and in the immortality of the soul. Most important of all, he needed God, in order to know which way he was going and what his destination was.

Tolstoy's relations with his God, whom he needed so much, were extremely vague. In the eighties the poet and novelist Aksakov said that Tolstoy had his own individual reckoning with God. In the 1900's Maxim Gorki, who had watched Tolstoy in the Crimea, wrote, "He has very vague relations with God. At times they remind me of the relations between two bears sharing a den."

The new phase of Tolstoy's spiritual development manifested itself in the weakening of his dogmatic attitude and in a growth of tolerance; the old proud and unshakable truths mellowed and were forgotten. He was suddenly able to write in his diary, "Only those periods of my life were happy during which I gave everything I have to the service of other people. Among them were the school, my work as arbitrator, my work during the famine, and religious guidance." According to his previous theories, every one of these activities was subject to severe criticism.

Tolstoy believed that he had long since conquered death through reasoning. During the eighties he had worked on his book "Life and Death." In the course of his work he reached the conclusion that a Christian could not die, and the book was published under the title *About Life*. Tolstoy reasoned that, after the death of the body, the immortal soul unites with "everything"—with God—and by liberating itself from the sinful body—its prison—begins a new phase of eternal life. During the next twenty or twenty-five years he tried in every way to convince himself that he was right. He hypnotized himself by constantly talking, writing, and thinking about eternal life. More than once he became aware of his restlessness, his inconsistencies, and his doubts. But whenever he dwelt on the problem of death, he wanted to believe that he had acquiesced, that he looked at it calmly, and that he was even ready for it.

Yet when he was at the point of death in the Crimea, the Countess wrote, "Every relapse depresses him: he becomes silent and moody. God alone knows what takes place in his soul. To us who are around him he is tender and grateful. He is not accustomed to being sick, and he suffers. I believe that he has no desire to die." Describing the same days, Maxim Gorki wrote, "At times the old sorcerer seemed to toy with death, flirt with it, and try to cheat it: 'I am not afraid of you, I love you, I am waiting for you.' At the same time his sharp eyes were asking: 'What does it look like? What is behind it? And beyond that? Will it destroy me completely, or will something remain? . . .'"

These harsh words seem to be a fair reflection of his attitude.

After Tolstoy had welcomed death in his diary, in his letters, and in his conversations, the entry which Gusev, his secretary, made in his diary on January 19, 1909, comes as a distinct surprise. Tolstoy, he wrote, said to him, "Today I suddenly felt death, which is only natural at my age, and I had no resistance. It was not a desire to die, which man sometimes feels when he realizes the futility of life and wants to escape it, but a complete calmness and resignation. This experience was entirely new to me."

During the last years of his life he admitted that he was still in search of truth, that he had much work ahead of him and many changes in his inner life.

Everything dogmatic and final became distasteful to him. He openly protested against "Tolstoyism," and occasionally said about his followers, "He is a Tolstoyan; that is, a man entirely foreign to my beliefs."

3

"The day will come when they will drag you to prison at the end of a rope!" the Countess warned her husband.

"That is all I want," he answered unflinchingly.

Tolstoy actually was eager to suffer for his convictions. He behaved in the most provoking manner. He never held back his opinions in the course of a conversation. His impassioned attacks on the state, the church, the principles of force, and private property were published abroad in Russian and in other languages. Thousands of copies of his pamphlets were distributed illegally throughout Russia. At intervals Tolstoy wrote letters to the Tsar. In a letter addressed to Nicholas II in 1902 he pictured —without temporizing—the dangerous internal situation of Russia, and the general discontent. Such articles as "Come to Your Senses!" written during the Russo-Japanese war, or "I Cannot Be Silent!" written during Stolypin's stern regime, created indignation in bureaucratic circles.

The government refused to touch Tolstoy.

In 1891 an energetic campaign directed against him was conducted in the conservative press in connection with one of his articles that had appeared in England. Government officials wanted to utilize this situation. In every report on church affairs, Pobyedonostzev persistently impressed on the Tsar the necessity of taking extraordinary measures against "the founder of a new heresy."

But the reactionary Alexander III remained adamant. In response to the pleas of the reactionaries he said, "I ask you not to touch Tolstoy! I have not the slightest intention of making a martyr of him and of directing the indignation of all Russia against me. If he is guilty, so much the worse for him."

Nicholas II adopted the same policy.

Tolstoy found himself in an unprecedented position. He was surrounded by police spies and detectives. The government watched his every step. Refusals to perform compulsory military service and distribution of antigovernment and antichurch literature could be traced to Yasnaya Polyana. An unwritten policy was followed of systematically persecuting all manifestations of Tolstoy's teachings, and all people responsible for spreading them. Prison, military prison, proscription, and loss of position were the lot of Tolstoy's followers and of the people close to him.

But Tolstoy invariably remained beyond the reach of the all-powerful police.

In the late nineties he addressed letters to the ministers of justice and of the interior. He notified them that he alone was responsible for the spread of "Tolstoyan" ideas, and announced that he would always continue to commit acts that the government considered sinful and which he considered his sacred duty before God. He tried to persuade the ministers to take extreme measures against him, to imprison him, to exile him, or worse. He wrote, "Most people will approve wholeheartedly of such action and will say: About time!"

His pleas remained unanswered. As more of his followers were punished, a sense of guilt, gratitude, even tenderness toward them crystallized within him. He tried to repay them with love and friendly assistance.

This sense of guilt and gratitude was an important factor in Tolstoy's attachment for Chertkov. Toward the end of 1896, Chertkov, Biryukov, and Tregubov wrote an appeal for help for the Dukhobors, who were being persecuted by the authorities in the Caucasus. Tolstoy signed the appeal along with the others. A number of copies were made, and sent to government officials and people prominent in public life. In the appeal the government was openly denounced, but even in this instance Tolstoy was not prosecuted. The other signers were subjected to arrest and exile. Chertkov was permitted to go abroad. After he settled in London, he organized the publishing house, "Svobodnoye Slovo." About a third of the work consisted of publishing such of Tolstoy's writings as had been barred by the Russian censorship. The rest consisted of publishing the writings of Chertkov and of his friends. The business was conducted in a casual way. A large capital was needed for printing and illegally transporting the books and magazines to Russia. A part of the money was donated, through Tolstoy, by various people. Another part was contributed to the treasury by Chertkov. Among the material published, only Tolstoy's works were of any value. The entire operation was not motivated by profit; however, it brought Chertkov to the fore as Tolstoy's only representative, as his personal friend, and as his literary agent.

Chertkov's labors in collecting, preserving, and publishing Tolstoy's works were in the latter's opinion the altruistic efforts of a friend. Added to this was a tender feeling for a man who had been subjected to persecution for openly espousing Tolstoy's ideas.

Chertkov had been Tolstoy's first important follower. He had satisfied the teacher's craving for a disciple. Under the pressure of spiritual experiences, amid all his changes and discoveries, Tolstoy valued the friendship of a man whose clear understanding of the Christian teachings could not be questioned. Tolstoy realized his own capacity for "running away" and for persisting in "peculiar stupidities." He considered it important to discuss his thoughts and theories with a pedantic and devoted follower. By asking pertinent questions, Chertkov helped Tolstoy to express his ideas. He could hold lengthy discussions with him about love for King Herod. These characteristics, together with Chertkov's ability to be pleasant when he chose, placed him in a unique position. Tolstoy insisted that Chertkov was indispensable.

The Countess said that in the late eighties Chertkov had already become a "collector"; for the purpose of "using" and "preserving" he systematically took possession of the original

Tolstoy manuscripts. Soon this became standard procedure, and every word Tolstoy wrote, after it had been copied, went as a matter of course to Chertkov. Later a staff of assistants gathered around him, and they assorted, classified, and edited the material.

After 1891, when Tolstoy had publicly relinquished his copyrights, he still retained the rights to the first editions, which could be the source of a large income. Chertkov was at the head of the publishing house "Posrednik," which needed capital for its development. Among other ways of raising capital, Chertkov used Tolstoy's manuscripts, which he published whenever he pleased. Thus Chertkov gradually acquired complete control of Tolstoy's works.

At first the Countess was friendly to Chertkov. True, she was jealous of him, and at times felt that he was alienating her husband from her, but she became accustomed to him and learned to accept him as a living example of all Tolstoyan ideals. She was indifferent to the fate of Tolstoy's religious and philosophical treatises, but when he returned to his literary work, she realized the size of the sums brought by the sale of first editions. Her desire to protect the family interests put her on her guard. By exercising pressure on her husband, she tried to take the publishing of first editions out of Chertkov's hands. To avoid arguments, Tolstoy, during the last few years of his life, decided not to publish anything he wrote, and much of his important work remained in manuscript.

In 1895 Tolstoy wrote his will in his diary. Among other provisions, he advised his heirs to refuse the royalties from his works. He worded this merely in the form of a plea.

He wrote, "If you will do so, good and well, it will be good for your sake; if you will not, that is your business—it means that you are not ready for it. The fact that my books have been sold during the last ten years has been one of the hardest things I had to face in life."

The page bearing his wishes was torn out of his diary, signed by Tolstoy, and preserved by his daughter Mary.

When, in 1902, the Countess accidentally learned about it, she persuaded her husband to give the paper to her for safekeeping. As soon as she received it she destroyed it, and was surprised at her daughter's indignation.

In her diary for October 10, 1902, the Countess wrote, "To consider Lev's writings public property, I think both bad and senseless. I love my family and wish for its well-being. If we were to give the writings to the public we would benefit only the rich publishing firms, such as Marx, Zetlin, and the others. I told Lev that should he die before me, I would not carry out his wishes and would not relinquish the royalties. If I had considered it fair and just, I would have relinquished them during his lifetime to please him, but after his death it would not make any sense."

She made these statements in an open and straightforward manner, but Tolstoy paid no attention to them.

In his will the sorting of his papers was entrusted to Chertkov. Apparently on Chertkov's initiative the question of the will arose again in 1904. In May, 1904, Tolstoy wrote to his friend in England a semiofficial letter in which he confirmed his wishes that in the future Chertkov and the Countess would examine and sort his papers, and would make whatever use of them they pleased. In the same letter Tolstoy mentioned that he attached no importance to the way in which these papers were used.

Temporarily other events crowded this question into the background.

In the autumn of 1906 the Countess became seriously ill. Terrible pains made her scream incessantly. The children gathered around her. Professor Snegirev arrived from Moscow and diagnosed a malignant internal growth. Much could have been said against an operation, but the moment arrived when the professor announced, "If the operation is not performed, the patient will die." Tolstoy was against an operation, which would interfere with the "great and magnificent act of death," but he refused to make the decision. The patient and the children gave their joint consent.

Professor Snegirev, toward whom Tolstoy behaved in a very

aloof manner, remembered how touching he was with his sick wife:

"On one occasion he said to the Countess: 'You are in bed; I cannot hear your footsteps in the rooms, and I find it difficult to read or write.'

"During the minutes he saw her immediately after the operation, an overwhelmingly touching tenderness was in his eyes and in his voice, though he joked with her as usual."

In the same year, a worse tragedy awaited Tolstoy. Late in November his daughter, Princess Mary Obolensky, died from typhoid fever in Yasnaya Polyana.

A month after her death Tolstoy wrote in his diary, "I live and frequently think of Mary's last moments. Seems strange to call her Mary—such a simple name is inadequate for the being who has left me! She is propped up with pillows on all sides, I am holding her thin, dear hand, and I feel that life is ebbing, that she is leaving me. This quarter-of-an-hour is one of the most important and significant in my entire life."

On August 28, 1908, Tolstoy was eighty years old. The public had begun to prepare for the celebration of this anniversary long in advance. Special committees were formed in the larger cities. The aged writer interrupted these preparations by making a public statement: he asked his friends not to hold any celebrations, which he found extremely disagreeable. All preparations were stopped, but for two weeks after his birthday an endless stream of congratulations poured into Yasnaya Polyana from all the ends of the earth. The Countess decided to take advantage of this opportune moment to bring out a new twenty-volume edition of Tolstoy's works. She hoped, by using her influential connections, to secure permission to include in this edition many of the works that had previously been barred by the censorship.

The estimated cost of the printing was between fifty and seventy thousand rubles.

In the meantime the family learned that some of the publish-

ing firms were willing to offer a million rubles in gold for the
exclusive rights to all of Tolstoy's writings.

The Countess consulted her lawyers and was advised that, on
the strength of the power of attorney she held, she could not
sell anything that had not been written. At the same time she
was told that Tolstoy's refusal to accept royalties on everything
he had written after 1881 would become inoperative after his
death, unless special stipulations prescribed by law were made
in his will.

In publishing, the Countess had to face the problem of protecting her edition against all the eventualities in case of Tolstoy's death.

A series of new quarrels ensued, and some very stormy scenes
took place in the presence of Chertkov. Apparently, Tolstoy's
wishes meant little to the Countess. She made no attempt to conceal the fact that, after his death, his works published since 1881
would not be in the public domain. Chertkov's work was in
jeopardy. Through unstinting efforts he had acquired undis-
puted control of everything Tolstoy had written since 1881,
but after Tolstoy's death the heirs would inherit all the rights.
To make certain that "Tolstoy's will" was carried out and to
assure Chertkov's position, a new will had to be drawn. Unquestionably, an appeal to the authority and powers of the state
was contrary to the conceptions of Christianity, as understood
by the "Tolstoyans." But this consideration had no effect on
Chertkov, though Tolstoy considered that his "clear understanding of the Christian teachings" could not be questioned. This
matter could not wait any longer. Any day could spell disaster.
Tolstoy was very old and became more and more apt to do anything to keep peace in the family.

Chertkov proceeded in a deliberate and methodical manner.
In September, 1909, the Tolstoys were visiting in his country
place, Krekshino. He chose a moment when no one else was
present and pointed out to Tolstoy that his children intended
to claim the rights that he wanted to bequeath to the public.
Tolstoy wrote in his diary, "I am loath to believe this." But next

day he signed a document which he called a will. Three of Chertkov's guests served as witnesses. In this document, Tolstoy reaffirmed his wish that such of his writings as had appeared since 1881 should remain in the public domain after his death. He also wrote, "I wish that all my manuscripts and papers be given to V. G. Chertkov, so that he can dispose of them after my death in the same manner in which he disposes of them now."

This paper was shown to an experienced lawyer, who expressed the opinion that it was insufficient.

Several meetings took place between Chertkov and his friends, and with the advice of the same lawyer a new will was made.

Chertkov decided to avoid the difficult position of a legal heir, and transferred the burden of all future conflicts on Tolstoy's youngest daughter, Countess Alexandra. As Chertkov expressed it, her role of official heir was only to "assure me the privilege of managing the literary estate of Count Tolstoy in accordance with the instructions he had given me and without undue interference." This idea was further elaborated in a codicil written by Chertkov and signed by Tolstoy.

At the meetings between Chertkov, his friends, and their lawyer, the formal text of the will was prepared and later submitted to Tolstoy. The Countess had no knowledge of this transaction.

In signing the document, Tolstoy said, "This entire business is most distasteful. We should not have to resort to questionable means in order to disseminate our thoughts. Christ, though I have no idea of comparing myself to Him, never had to worry that someone would claim His thoughts as His personal property. He never even put them down in writing. Instead He expressed them courageously, and went to the cross for them. His thoughts never disappeared. A word cannot disappear if it expresses truth, and if the man who utters it steadfastly believes in its truthfulness. The necessity for such artificial measures is the result of our lack of faith in what we profess."

Chertkov's emissary disagreed. Among other things he said, "I will not conceal from you how much your friends were hurt when they had to listen to the accusation that, though you denied the right to own land, you had transferred the title to your estate to your wife and children. We shall be hurt just as much when we are told that, though Tolstoy knew that his public declaration of 1891 had no standing in the courts, he took no steps to see that his wishes would be carried out and in that way helped to convey his copyrights to his family. I cannot begin to tell you how painful this will be to your friends."

This argument struck home. Tolstoy had long since expressed his regrets that he had transferred his property to the family. He believed that the money had done a great deal of harm to individual members of it.

Tolstoy took a walk, considered what Chertkov had to say, and decided to will to Countess Alexandra, for disposition by Chertkov, all his works, including those written before 1881 and which were being published by his wife for the benefit of the family.

This was more than Chertkov had expected. In praising Tolstoy for taking such a decisive step, he reminded him that his family considered his books written before 1881 as their property.

Tolstoy paid no attention and after several abortive attempts finally rewrote and signed the new will on July 22, 1910. He executed the document secretly, in a forest thicket. Chertkov's friend, the pianist Goldenweiser, and two of his employees served as witnesses.

The relations between the Countess and Chertkov frequently became strained. Tolstoy never tired of saying that Chertkov was "indispensable." Among wives, antagonism toward the friends of the husband is not an uncommon occurrence. The Countess had always been jealous. She felt that her role in history was to appear in the eyes of contemporaries and of future generations as a kind fairy protecting the talent and health of her genius husband. The appearance of the "indispensable" man interfered with her dreams. As years went by, her disposition became more despotic, irritable, and violent. Sometimes she believed that the approaches to her husband's soul were blocked by Chertkov, who had forced his way into their family life. He seemed to be taking her husband away from her. But these attacks of jealousy passed, and the Countess made herself suppress any show of ill-feeling. Eight years of Chertkov's enforced absence in England allayed the feeling of jealousy in the Countess. In 1908, during a family gathering, she drank Chertkov's health, and said that she considered him the "best friend of the family." In 1909, with her husband, she visited the Chertkovs in Krekshino.

The time came when the Countess began to sense a conspiracy around her. Tolstoy became secretive. Her youngest daughter, Countess Alexandra, was an independent, grown person who adored her father. Following the example of her older sisters, she had learned shorthand, and helped him in his work. From an early age, Alexandra Tolstoy was energetic, full of initiative, and self-willed. In defending her father, she sided against her mother. Countess Alexandra and her friends who served as typists in Yasnaya Polyana formed what might be termed the Tolstoy clique. Behind them stood Chertkov, the musician Goldenweiser, and other intimate friends of Tolstoy's. The Countess was alone. Her only backing came from her two youngest sons, who shared her antagonistic attitude toward Tolstoy's ideas, her concern about the estate, and her aversion for Chertkov, but they seldom came to Yasnaya Polyana.

These two warring camps besieged the rapidly aging and peacefully minded Tolstoy and were tearing him apart.

The Countess insisted that everything was being concealed from her: conversations, interviews, letters, exchange of papers between her daughter Alexandra and Chertkov's secretaries—a situation which had never existed during her long married life. There must be a reason for this. Everything around her aroused her fears and suspicions.

Financial considerations played a certain part in her state of mind. The family, which she loved above everything else, consisted of twenty-eight people, counting the grandchildren. Their security depended to a great extent on the nature of Tolstoy's will. A million rubles was at stake. The fate of the new twenty-volume edition also added to her worries.

At last the Countess could no longer stand the strain. On June 22, 1910, Tolstoy, who was visiting Chertkov, received a disturbing telegram from his wife and returned to Yasnaya Polyana. He found her in a terrible condition. She had suffered a nervous breakdown. Chertkov denied that she was ill, but the evidence was on her side. The Countess was sixty-five. She had lived through forty-eight strenuous and nerve-racking years of married life, and through thirteen births. Even in 1906, Professor Snegirev had doubted the wisdom of operating, because of the poor condition of her nervous system. In June, 1910, two doctors were invited to Yasnaya Polyana: the specialist, Professor Rossolimo, and Dr. Nikitin, a splendid physician who had known the Countess for a long time. After examining and observing her for two days they made a diagnosis: "Degenerative double personality; paranoiac and hysterical, chiefly the former." At the moment she was having a temporary relapse.

The tragic situation was made worse because the unquestionable symptoms of the illness were interwoven with natural jealousy, hatred, and financial worries. Chertkov and his friends saw only malicious pretense, and demanded that Tolstoy stand his ground, but Tolstoy thought differently. On August 14, 1910, he wrote in his diary:

"I know that her present condition may seem like deliberate pretense, and partly this may be true, but the fact of the illness remains—of a very real illness, which deprives her of her will and of her self-control. If I were to say that she alone is responsible for this lack of will and self-indulgence which began a long time ago, I must forget that this is an old sin. Now she is not responsible. I cannot feel anything except pity for her and I cannot—at least I find it absolutely impossible—to contradict her and augment her suffering. I know that defending my decision, which is contrary to her wishes, is bad for her, and even if I believed otherwise, I should not have the heart to argue with her."

He attempted to reason with both sides and begged them "not to exaggerate."

To Chertkov he wrote, "Often she is very pitiful to me. When I think how alone she must feel during the nights, most of which she is sleepless, and how, with a hazy, sickly awareness, she realizes that she is not loved and is a burden to everyone except the children, I cannot help feeling sorry for her."

He said, "Some people, like Alexandra, want to explain everything away by calling it greed, but this is much more complicated: back of it are forty years of married life and that means habit, pride, jealousy, illness. . . . At times her condition is pitiful."

Tolstoy's diaries, some of which were in Chertkov's possession, were the cause of the first major quarrel. In a warm letter the Countess asked Chertkov to return the diaries; he answered with a blunt refusal. During the hysterical scenes that followed, Chertkov was harsh. She demanded that their house be closed to Chertkov. About the middle of July she guessed that a new will was in existence.

After that, the Tolstoy household and the gay and happy Yasnaya Polyana were plunged into a living hell. The unfortunate woman lost the last vestiges of self-control. She eavesdropped, she spied, she tried not to let her husband out of her sight for a minute, she went through his papers in search of the will or for some reference to herself or to Chertkov. She was no longer able to be fair with the people around her. Time and again she threw herself at Tolstoy's feet and begged him to tell her whether a new will existed. She rolled on the floor in hysterics, she tried to shoot herself, she carried a bottle of opium and constantly threatened to take her life if this or that whim were not obeyed instantly.

The life of the eighty-two-year-old Tolstoy became unbearable. The secretly made will preyed on his conscience. He found himself standing between an abnormal wife and her adversaries, who were ready to accuse the sick woman of every imaginable crime.

Her threats, though they were almost a daily occurrence, kept him in a state of terrific tension. He exclaimed, "Just imagine these threats of suicide! . . . At times they are empty words, but who knows? . . . Just imagine if it should happen! . . . What shall I do if I have that on my conscience?"

An example of how violent and hateful the struggle was around the apostle of love and truth is found in a letter from Chertkov to Tolstoy, dated July 27, 1910:

"Dear Friend,

"I have just seen Countess Alexandra who told me about everything that is happening to you. She knows more because there is no pretense in her presence and she can see certain things that are concealed from you. . . .

"The sad truth, which we have to tell you, is that all the scenes that have taken place within the last two weeks and the arrival of Lev and Andrew have only one definite and practical reason. If these scenes were accompanied by certain real symptoms of illness—and that would not be surprising after such an extended, strenuous, and tiresome pretense!—then these symptoms were exploited cleverly with the same end in view.

"This purpose is to estrange you from me and, if possible, from Countess Alexandra, and to learn from you by constant, combined pressure whether you have signed a will that deprives your family of your literary estate; if you have not signed it, then by keeping you under constant observation until your death to prevent you from doing so; if you have already signed it, then not to let you go anywhere until they have had time to invite reactionary doctors who, in order to nullify your will, can pronounce you of unsound mind because of old age."

Tolstoy was plunged into a deep controversy, which disgusted him and which was carried on by people who were dear to him. He could not breathe, and he was losing his strength. At last, on October 3, he had a serious attack, accompanied by convulsions. The Countess rose to the emergency. She helped the doctor and the children around the bed of her dying husband. Later she threw herself on her knees, embraced his feet, laid her head on them, and for a long time remained in that position.

She was a tragic figure. As she sat at the sick man's side, or as she wandered through the rooms, she lifted her eyes, hurriedly made numerous signs of the cross, and whispered, "Oh, Lord! Only not now, not this time! . . ."

To Countess Alexandra she said, "I am suffering more than you: you are losing your father, while I am losing my husband, for whose death I am to blame! . . ."

According to a number of impartial witnesses, her fear and suffering were sincere.

But no one can guess what takes place in the human heart. While the situation was still critical, the Countess found time to take a briefcase filled with papers from her husband's desk.

Her eldest daughter stopped her: "Mama, why did you take the briefcase?"

"So Chertkov would not get it."

Tolstoy recovered, but he was noticeably weaker; he sensed his approaching death, and he thought more and more frequently about leaving the "lunatic asylum" vibrating with emotion and hatred. He had an irresistible urge to die in peace, away from people "who have exchanged me for rubles."

Toward the end of October, talking to Novikov, a peasant whom he had known for a long time, he said, "I am stewing in this house as I would in hell. Yes, yes! believe me, I am sincere with you! I will not die in this house. I have decided to leave for some unknown place where no one knows me. Perhaps I shall come to your house to die. . . . I have not left, I could not leave before for selfish reasons, but now I see that my departure will be good for the family. There will be fewer arguments, and they will sin less."

On October 24, Tolstoy wrote to Novikov and asked whether he could rent a small, warm house in his neighborhood in case he decided to leave Yasnaya Polyana.

And still Tolstoy wavered and hesitated. The Countess had firmly and solemnly promised she would take her life on the day he left.

4

On October 28, Tolstoy awoke at three in the morning. As on preceding nights, he heard stealthy steps and doors being opened and closed. He peered in the direction of his study, and saw a bright light. He heard the rustle of paper and realized that the Countess was searching his desk. Only the day before, she had demanded that he leave the doors unlocked. Both of her doors were always open, so that she could hear his slightest movement. Night and day his every word had to be known to her, his every move seen by her eyes. Again he heard the study door being opened and her steps as she walked by. An overwhelming feeling of revulsion and indignation took possession of him. He acutely felt the falseness and the shamefulness of his position.

He tried to sleep but to no avail. For an hour he twisted in bed, then he lighted a candle. Instantly the Countess appeared and asked how he was.

His revulsion and indignation were mounting. His breath came in gasps. He counted his pulse: ninety-seven. He could not stay in bed, and suddenly a firm and final decision matured within him.

Quickly he wrote a letter to his wife and began to pack. Then he awoke his daughter Alexandra, a friend who was staying with her, and Dushan Makovitsky, the doctor.

Gently Tolstoy tiptoed over and closed the doors of his wife's bedroom as well as the doors leading into the hall.

He was in a panic: "Quiet, quiet, no noise!" He trembled whenever he thought that his wife would hear him, that she would become hysterical, and that he would not be able to leave without a scene.

They moved quietly, without saying a word. Packing was difficult: his hands trembled, the straps refused to snap, the suit-case would not close.

A little after five he went to the stables to arouse the men and give orders to harness the horses. The night was very dark. He stepped off the path into the underbrush, scratched himself, stumbled against a tree, fell, lost his hat, could not find his way, and with difficulty returned to the house. His daughter found another hat, and by the light of an electric torch they dragged the suitcase to the stable. The men were awake, the horses harnessed. Hurriedly, Tolstoy put the bridles on the horses; he was trembling, expecting pursuit any moment. At last everything was ready. The stable boy, with a torch in his hand, mounted a horse. The coach followed him along the drive around the house.

On that dark night the trembling, eighty-two-year-old Tolstoy escaped from Yasnaya Polyana, never to return.

His only companion was his friend Dr. Makovitsky.

About eleven in the morning steps were heard in the Countess's bedroom. Her daughter came into the living room to meet her. In a frightened voice the Countess asked, "Where is Papa?"

"Father has gone away."

"Where?"

"I have no idea."

"What do you mean you have no idea? Has he gone forever?"

"He left a letter for you. Here it is."

The Countess quickly took the letter, and glanced at the contents. Tolstoy had written:

"4 A.M. October 28, 1910

"My departure will be bitter news for you and I am sorry, but please understand and believe when I say that I could not have done anything else. My position in the house has become unbearable. In addition to everything else, I can no longer live in the luxurious surroundings in which I have been living, and I am doing what old men of my age should do: I am leaving mundane affairs so I can spend the remaining days of my life in peace and solitude. If you learn where I am, please understand and do not come after me. Your arrival would only make our situation more difficult without altering my decision. I am grateful to you for the forty-eight years of honest life you have spent with me, and I ask you to forgive me for everything I have done to you, just as I am forgiving you from the bottom of my heart for anything you might have done to me. I hope you will accept the new position in which my departure places you and will not harbor any ill-will for me. If you wish to communicate with me, speak to Alexandra. She will know where I am and will forward anything important. She cannot tell where I am because I have made her promise not to reveal my whereabouts to anyone.

"LEV TOLSTOY"

"He has left! . . . He has left forever! . . ." the Countess screamed. "I cannot live without him! . . . I will drown myself!"

She threw the letter on the floor and, wearing only a dress, ran out of the house in the direction of the pond. Her daughter, Tolstoy's secretary Bulgakov, and the servants ran after her.

The Countess reached the float that was used for laundering, slipped, fell, and rolled into a shallow spot in the pond. She sank at once.

Her daughter jumped in after her. Standing up to her waist in water, she pulled her mother up, and passed her into the hands of people on the float.

In the course of the terrible day the Countess tried more than once to run to the pond but she was watched, and forcibly restrained. She cried incessantly, beat her breast with a paperweight and with a hammer, tried to stab herself with a knife and with scissors, and finally tried to jump out of the window.

All through the night she wandered from room to room, alternating long silences with loud sobs.

Toward evening, a doctor and a nurse arrived from Tula. Next day, the entire family gathered in Yasnaya Polyana.

In the meantime, Tolstoy reached the convent in which his sister was a nun. Here, unexpectedly, he was joined by his youngest daughter and her friend. Afraid that his whereabouts would become known, he prepared to move at once. They decided to go to Novocherkassk, where a relative of the Tolstoys was working, to attempt to secure foreign passports and to go somewhere abroad—not to any of the larger countries of Western Europe, but to some place like Bulgaria.

Tolstoy's companions discussed their destination and the best routes. Pathetically weak, he swayed on his feet and only urged them to continue the flight and to escape pursuit.

"Enough, enough!" he said. "We will not join any colony, and we will avoid any acquaintances. I want the simple life of a peasant."

"Will you suffer remorse and accuse yourself if anything should happen to mother?"

"Certainly not," he answered. "A person cannot suffer with remorse over a situation in which he has no choice. But should something happen to her, I shall suffer . . . I shall suffer very much."

He believed that the time had come, not for his own salvation, but for the salvation of human dignity and of the spark of God that had been endangered by his life in Yasnaya Polyana.

He exchanged letters with his wife. Her last letter cannot be read without a feeling of deep compassion for a pitiful, crushed woman, who was at a loss what to say. She still hoped, begged for mercy, protested that she loved him, promised, and tried to persuade.

Tolstoy wrote to her that another meeting between them would be terrible. He believed that she was sincere, but he thought that she was not in a condition to carry out her promises.

While running away from the possibility of a pursuit, he constantly thought and tried to find some way out of their situation, and could not think of anything. But fate was already preparing a way out. He was taken ill in a railroad coach. They had to leave the train at the large railroad station of Astapovo.

The station master placed his house at the sick man's disposal.
Tolstoy had contracted pneumonia, which is fatal to so many old
people.

On November 7, 1910, he died, surrounded by love, tenderness, and the painstaking care of a number of doctors. His friend
Chertkov, his two daughters, and his eldest son were with him
at the end. When his condition was already serious, he dictated
a telegram to his younger sons, "Condition better, but heart so
weak that meeting Mama would be fatal for me."

Above all else he feared that his whereabouts would become
known, and that he would have to face the Countess.

Once he looked at his eldest daughter, who was sitting by his
bed, and quietly said, "Much will fall on Sonya."

Tatyana could not hear him, and he repeated, "Much . . .
much will fall on Sonya . . . arranged things badly."

Then he said something she could not understand.

"Would you like to see her? Would you like to see Sonya?"

He was silent.

In the delirium he screamed, "To escape . . . to escape . . .
they will catch me . . ."

In the meantime the railroad station at Astapovo became
crowded with reporters. The telegraph was working day and
night, carrying news of Tolstoy's condition all over the world.
On a sidetrack stood a special train in which the Countess and
the younger members of the family were living. She had been
persuaded not to enter Tolstoy's room until he was well.

Leaning on the arm of one of her sons, she walked to the station master's little house and fixed her eyes on her husband's
windows. In one of the other rooms a window opened, and the
latest news was given her. She stood silently for some time, then
quietly returned to the train, and only in the privacy of the car
gave vent to her tears.

The Countess wrote, "The doctors admitted me only when he
was barely breathing, lying motionless and with eyes already
closed. Quietly, tenderly, still hoping that he would hear me,
I whispered in his ear that I had been in Astapovo all the time,

and that I loved him until the end. . . . I cannot remember what else I said, but for an answer I received two deep sighs, as if a terrific effort were behind them, and then everything became quiet."

During his illness Tolstoy endured severe physical pain, but he was gentle and exceptionally loving with those who were near him. He became excited and irritated only when the person on duty by his bed could not take down or understand the thoughts that he vainly attempted to dictate.

More than once he whispered, "Seek! always seek! . . ."

Such words as could be distinguished were taken down, but no one knows what he thought during the days and nights that he spent in Astapovo. Apparently, he could discern the approaching end, and death, which he had called so ardently during his last years, seemed heavy and oppressive. He had no desire to die, but everything happened so much more simply than he had once imagined.

Countess Alexandra's friend walked into the room. Suddenly he rose in bed, stretched out his hands to her, and in a loud, gay voice cried, "Mary! Mary!"

He seemed to have expected to see his favorite daughter, who had died four years before.

His last breath came calmly.

Eight years later, in connection with the publication of Tolstoy's works, I had to spend several days in Yasnaya Polyana. The Countess and her youngest daughter were already reconciled. Calm and weary, she met me with a great deal of dignity. She was seventy-four years old, tall, slightly stooped, very thin, and she moved through the rooms like a shadow, which a gust of wind could carry away. Every day she walked a mile to her husband's grave to decorate it with fresh flowers.

I walked with her to the grave. Tolstoy is buried in a distant corner of the park, on the edge of a ravine, under tall, spreading trees. A wooden fence surrounds the small mound of earth, and inside stands a plain bench. Everything was quiet in that peaceful spot. Sad thoughts were stirred only by the whisper of the leaves above our heads.

The Countess talked willingly but without a smile. With evident relish, she read aloud her recollections of the happy days in Yasnaya Polyana. She recited from memory several poems dedicated to her by Fet. She spoke about Chertkov without anger but with cold animosity.

Her remarks about the last ten years of her life with her husband were not always kind.

She was silent for several seconds and then said:

"Yes, I lived with Lev for forty-eight years but I never really learned what kind of a man he was. . . ."

Index

Books That Live

The Norton imprint on a
book means that in the
publisher's estimation it
is a book not for a single
season but for the years.

W · W · NORTON & CO · INC.

70 FIFTH AVENUE

NEW YORK